Gil Scott-Heron was born in Chicago in 1949. He has been opening eyes, minds and souls for thirty years. A highly influential and widely admired singer, proto-rapper, jazz pianist, published poet, novelist and socio-political commentator, Scott-Heron remains a unique and major figure in global music. With over fifteen albums to his name, his politically charged output has won him an international following. His work illuminates a philosophy of life that holds human affection as well as political and artistic responsibility as the underlying factors that inspire his writing. The publication of *Now and Then* – the first ever British issue of his poetry – is a major deal. For real.

THE POEMS OF
GIL SCOTT-HERON

PAYBACK PRESS / BROUHAHA BOOKS

First published in the UK in 2000 by Payback Press, an imprint of
Canongate Books Ltd, 14 High Street, Edinburgh EH1 1TE, Scotland

Published simultaneously in the
United States of America and Canada
in 2001 by Payback Press

10 9 8 7 6 5 4 3 2

Parts of this collection have previously been published in the
United States of America as *So Far, So Good*, Third World Press, 1990

British Library Cataloguing-in-Publication Data
A catalogue record for this book is available on request
from the British Library

ISBN 0 86241 900 X

Typeset by Hewer Text Ltd, Edinburgh
Printed and bound by WS Bookwell, Finland

Gil would like to thank Bingo, Whitney, Marley and Leo,
and also Peter Collingridge

NOW AND THEN

'This book is dedicated to my favourite critic, to my source of continuous joy and inspiration, the person I would most want to be like when I grow up. She lived and taught me how to live until November 1, 1999. I will always love you, mama.'

PRE-NOTES ON NOTES TO COME

be no bargain-day xtras on freedom and
ain't nobody givin it away.
echoes from overloud voices get rapped inside
badass black thunderclouds and carried to God who sits at
the corner of forever.
God sent down correctly.
God sent down right on timely:
music – muzak – muzick
soulfulsoothings soulfulmournings
messages that cannot be decoded by stale brains
bluesgospeljazzrhythmscreaminshouting-blasting serene
words and notes that mean:
inside you is where life is and not at woolworthless 5&10.
the message is here: inside the man
bubbling brain cells and heart/soul cells
ax-cell-er-rating faster until understood
and used and passed on and used and passed on and used
and . . .

Gil Scott-Heron
May 3rd 1971
[from *Pieces of a Man* liner notes]

CONTENTS

Contents

INTRODUCTION

WORDS ARE FOR THE MIND

Life inevitably translates into time. That is why the sum total of it is called 'a lifetime'. Freedom is the potential to spend one's time in any fashion one determines. I would always want the time invested in my ideas to be profitable, to give the reader something lasting for their investment in me. It is very important to me that my ideas be understood. It is not as important that *I* be understood. I believe that this is a matter of respect; your most significant asset is your time and your commitment to invest a portion of it considering my ideas means it is worth a sincere attempt on my part to transmit the essence of the idea. If you are looking, I want to make sure that there is something here for you to find.

The public 'lifetime' of an artist is comparable to that of an athlete – about five years. From the thousands of individuals who consider themselves candidates for visibility and public notice, few 'make it'. I have been blessed by the grace of 'the spirits' with the public's attention for nearly six of those lifetimes – songs that I've sung and poems that I've written have been heard on every continent, in every country where people have records and books. How could I possibly complain?

This is an 'overlapping collection'. It necessarily contains a number of poems that appeared in *So Far, So Good* and a few from *Small Talk at 125th and Lenox.* I say 'necessarily' because their inclusion satisfies the requests of people who have asked for the written text of poems from albums, and also gives me a chance to share poems that I feel are worthwhile but were not recorded. Even if you have heard these pieces sung or recited

xiii

in the past, reading these poems may offer you a fresh perspective on some of my ideas.

You don't think that rap is a brand new style?
No. In fact folks been rapping for a good little while.

Which brings us to why I am reluctant to accept the title of 'Godfather of Rap'. There still seems to be a need within our community to have what the *griot* supplied in terms of historical chronology; a way to identify and classify events in black culture that were both historically influential and still relevant. In basketball for example, Michael Jordan was the first 'Skywalker' unless you'd seen David Thompson. Dr. 'J' was the only 'Surgeon and General' who could rebound like a center, take the ball full court like a guard and dunk like nobody's business – unless you'd seen Connie Hawkins. In the same way, there were poets before me who had great influence on the language and the way it was performed and recorded: Oscar Brown Jr, Melvin Van Peebles and Amiri Baraka (a.k.a. LeRoi Jones) were all published and well respected for their poetry, plays, songs and a range of other artistic achievements when the only thing I was taping were my ankles before basketball practice. It was The Last Poets (both groups), and their percussion-driven group deliveries, who made the recordings which serve to place my title as 'Godfather' in question. If there was any individual initiative that I was responsible for it might have been that there was music in certain poems of mine, with complete progressions and repeating 'hooks', which made them more like songs than just recitations with percussion. I put this down to my background as a piano player prior to my attempts as a songwriter or to writing poems that could be performed in a musical setting.

The character of those pieces, particularly the early ones, brought about descriptions and analyses from journalists and critics that not only took in the metric and rhythmic values of them as poems or songs, but stumbled to conclusions about our philosophy. Because there were political elements in a few numbers, handy political labels were slapped across the body of our work, labels that maintain their innuendo of disapproval to this day. Words like 'radical' and 'militant' and 'muckraker' stuck out in the reviews like weeds in a rose garden. Those terms were amusing at first because we had no idea that they were 'terminal'. We attributed them to idiots under the pressure of editor-inspired deadlines who had not bothered with the words, but responded only to the street-sound drumbeats that sounded as if they were calling for the revolution that so many journalists in the late '60s thought would bring the end of the world.

So if it ain't exactly rap, and it ain't radical militant muckraking, what is it? Because of the contributions of Ron Carter and Hubert Laws on *Pieces of a Man* and the background of Bob Thiele, the owner-producer of The Flying Dutchman record label as a 'jazz' producer, Brian Jackson and I became 'jazz' artists. It certainly couldn't have been because of guitarist Bert Jones or drummer Bernard Purdie, and I doubt if it was because of 'The Revolution Will Not Be Televised' or 'Save the Children'.

I felt awkward with the 'jazz' label because that associated my efforts at song-writing and piano-playing with Duke Ellington and Miles Davis and Dolphy and Coltrane and . . . you dig? The closest I thought I would ever get to them was with the song 'Lady Day and John Coltrane', an up-tempo blues tribute to two of my favorite musicians. It was enough to make you think that if you wrote a hymn you got an automatic one-way ticket to heaven.

So what did we have in total? A militant-radical-muckraker? That's a great deal of description without even the briefest inference that there might be a piano player in the house. Rarely and barely one word about 'I Think I'll Call it Morning' or 'Save the Children' or 'Give Her a Call'.

I must also admit that some of my poetic ideas have not been all my own. I rarely wrote lyrics for Brian Jackson melodies without Brian giving me a point of reference for direction. There were also times when I ran into places along the song's road that I could not navigate, and lines that completed verses and supports for bridges were 'given to me'. By 'spirits'. The lyrics were 'blessings'. For me these songs became 'spirituals'.

I have been blessed because I have had the opportunity to do what I enjoy and find it to be something that others enjoy also. Many of my favorite ideas are here. It is kind of you to take an interest. I hope that you enjoy them as much as I have enjoyed preparing them to be shared. I do hope you enjoy these things that I have been taught along the way. They are the most valuable things I have.

They represent hours of concentration
And seconds of spiritual inspiration
With most of the beauty that I have seen
And what I have learned about what it all means
To be lifted by 'the spirits' and touched from within
To a place I can smile inside 'now and then'

Gil Scott-Heron
November 3rd 1998

I have no idea how many times I've been asked what I call my music, or how many jokes I have thought up to substitute for a serious answer – 'I call it collect', I might say, 'I call it mine', was another.

Collectively, at various times, we have called what we did *Midnight Music, Third World Music,* and *Bluesology.* Seriously trying to define it I've said it is *Black* music or *Black American* music. Because *Black Americans* are now a tremendously diverse essence of all the places we've come from and the music and rhythms we brought with us. And it has been our way of paying tribute and offering respect that we have included the many facets of our community.

But what do you call reggae, blues, african vibration, jazz, salsa, chants and poetry?

In truth I call what I have been granted the opportunity to share 'Gifts'. I would like to personally claim to be the source of the melodies and ideas that have come through me, but that is just the point. Many of the shapes of sound and concepts have come upon me from no place I can trace, notes and chords I'd never learned, thoughts and pictures I'd never seen – and all as clear as a sky untouched by cloud or smog or smoke or haze. Suddenly. Magically. As if transferred to me without effort.

My blessings have not just been words and notes. Not just art. My life has been blessed. With the joy of my children with the strength of my family with the opportunity to share something of great value that has brought a great number of people both pride and pleasure.

They have been gifts from the Spirits – so perhaps these songs and poems are 'spirituals'.

Don't ever let the spirits die.

Gil Scott-Heron
November 1993 [from *Spirits* liner notes]

xvii

COMING FROM A BROKEN HOME

I want to make this a special tribute
since I am a primary tributary and
a contributary, as it were,
to a family that contradicts the concepts,
heard the rules but wouldn't accept,
and womenfolk raised me and I was full grown
before I knew I came from a broken home.
Oh yeah!
Sent to live with my Grandma down south
[wonder why they call it down if the world is round]
where my uncle was leavin'
and my grandfather had just left for heaven, they said,
and as every ologist would certainly note
I had NO STRONG MALE FIGURE! RIGHT?
But Lily Scott was absolutely not
your mail order, room service, typecast Black grandmother.
On tiptoe she might have been five foot two
and in an overcoat 110 pounds, light
and light skin 'cause she was half-white
from Alabama and Georgia and Florida
and Africa.

Lily Scott claimed to have gone as far as the 3rd grade
in school herself,
put four Scotts through college
with her husband going blind.
[God rest his soul. A good man, Bob Scott]
And I'm talkin' 'bout work!
Lily worked through them teens
and them twenties
and them thirties and forties

1

and put four, all four of hers,
through college
and pulled and pushed and coaxed
folks all around her through and over other things.
I was moved in with her.
Temporarily.
Just until things was patched.
'Til this was patched
and 'til that was patched.
Until I became at
3,4,5,6,7,8,9 and 10
the patch
that held Lily Scott
who held me
and like them four
I became one more.
And I loved her from the absolute marrow of my bones
and we was holding on.
I come from a broken home.

She could take hers and outdo yours
or take yours and outdo hers.
She may not have been in a class by herself
but it sho' didn't take long to call the roll.
She had more than the five senses
knew more than books could teach
and raised everyone she touched just a little bit higher.
Common sense became uncommon
and you could sense that she had it.
And all around her
there was a natural sense,

as though she sensed
what the stars say
what the birds say
what the wind and the clouds say
a sense of soul and self,
that African sense.
'And work like you're building
something of your own,' she'd say.
Full time. Over time. All the time.
No nonsense.
And she raised me like she raised four of her own
who were like her
in a good many good ways.
Which showed up in my mother
who was truly her mother's daughter
and still her own person.
And I was hurt and scared and shocked
when Lily Scott left suddenly one night,
and they sent a limousine from heaven
to take her to God if there is one.
So I knew she had gone.
And I came from a broken home.

So on the streets of New York
the family, me and my mother,
moved on through my teens
where all the ologists'
hypothetical theoretical
analytical hypocritical
will not be able to factor
why I failed to commit

3

the obligatory robbery, burglary,
murder or rape.
Nor know that I was
fighting my way out of the ghetto.
But I lived in the projects without becoming one,
shot jumpers in the park
instead of people,
went to a school that
informed instead of reformed
read books without getting booked
and had a couple of jobs
to help with the surgery on my broken home.

And so my life has been guided
and all the love I needed was provided
and through my mother's sacrifices I saw where her life went
to give more than birth to me, but life to me.
And this ain't one of them clichés
about Black women being strong
'cause hell! If you're weak, you're gone!
But life courage, determined to do more than just survive.
Say what? Of course she had a choice:
Don't do it! Work.
Raining cold mornings, dirty streets
and dirty Goddamn people
worrying her way up rickety-ass stairs
working for Welfare . . .
I'm sorry if I'm drifting on
but this is all I know about a broken home:
And she sings better than I do
and I listen to her and B.B. manhandle Handel. [Joke]

4

And hey amigo!
17th and 8th in the park.
13th and 9th in the dark:
congas, cowbells, bongoes and salsa,
beer cans, Ripple and good herbs.
Willie Bobo, Eddie Palmieri, Ray Barreto
and the Mayor of my neighborhood
long before he covered 'The Bottle,' Joe Bataan.
Mi madre estudia in
La Universidad de San Juan
y vivia en San Turce
y mi madre vivia en Barranquitas

Yeah. Raised by women,
but they were not alone
because the chain of truth was not broken
in Bob Scott's home.
And my mother's name is Bob, Robert,
Bobbie Scott-Heron
and saying thank you, I love you ain't enough.

My life has been balanced on that razor's edge of God's
                                        rolling dice
and it seemed as though they had a job for me to do:
Because the Rambler got totalled in Avondale and
Geoffrey's Ford four o'clock soloing
through a D.C. slalom when the brakes locked
steel and wheels à la lamppost.
Good morning!
And the white preacher, Reverend Cockcroft,
who grabbed me when I treaded on the bottom of Lake
                                        Kiamesha.

5

And I am small remembering how
she showed me more caring and sharing than I deserved;
more courage and daring than I have.
The ONLY ONE who has ALWAYS been on my side.
And too many homes have a missing woman or man
without the feeling of missing love.
Maybe there are homes that are hurt,
but there are no REAL LIVES that hurt will not reach.
But not broken.
Unless the homes of soldiers stationed overseas
or lost in battles are broken.
Unless the homes of firemen, policemen, construction
                                                        workers,
seamen, railroad men, truckers, pilots who lost their lives,
but not what their lives stood for.
Because men die, lose, are lost and leave.
And so do women.
I come from WHAT THEY CALLED A BROKEN HOME,
but if they had ever really called at our house
they would have known how wrong they were.
We were working on our lives
and our homes and dealing with what we had,
not what we didn't have.
My life has been guided by women
but because of them I am a Man.
God bless you, Mama. And thank you.

In February 1981, I went on a *Black History Month* tour that took me to some of the nation's most prominent campuses and communities.

There were two things in particular that people everywhere wanted to talk about: First, I had just completed a most enjoyable and successful four-month tour with the #1 entertainer-composer-musician Stevie Wonder, which had included, on January 15th, a rally in Washington, D.C. in support of Dr. King's birthday becoming a national holiday.

'What were the chances? How many people were REALLY there? What sort of a brother was Stevie to just be around?'

Second, what were my feelings about the election of President Reagan?

Discussions concerning the second question started to become my first topic during the February lectures. A description of the conditions that paved the way for Mr. Reagan's election AND what I viewed as the conditions created by his victory.

In April, while working with a man I also consider a creative genius, musician-engineer Malcolm Cecil, the idea of recording the poem ('Part Two') without setting the stage, so to speak (with an introduction), didn't feel right. And there was also a line from a tune I kept hearing that I felt needed to be included:

'This ain't really your life, ain't really your life, ain't really, ain't really nothing but a movie.' The tune became 'Part Three' on the album *Reflections*.

And armed with a bunch of words, a vague structure and my ace-in-the-studio, Malcolm, 'B Movie' was born.

And, in 1984 when it became clear that the President would be running again, it was time for another round. However, I felt as though my friends, and even my enemies, would be let down if we decided to do 'B Movie II', or even 'B Movie Also (Too)'. I was glad to find that art can imitate art, even when 'it ain't really your life' – which is why II, 2 or TOO became 'Re-Ron'.

PART ONE

'B' MOVIE *INTRODUCTION*

The first thing I want to say is 'Mandate, my ass!'

Because it seems as though we've been convinced that 26% of the registered voters, not even 26% of the American people, but 26% of the registered voters form a mandate, or a landslide. 21% voted for 'Skippy' and 3 or 4% voted for someone else who might have been running.

And yes I do remember (in this year that we have declared to be from 'Shogun to Raygun'), I remember what I said about Raygun: 'I called him "Hollyweird". Acted like an actor. Acted like a liberal. Acted like General Franco when he acted like Governor of California. That's after he started acting like a Republican. Then (in 1976) acted like somebody was going to vote for him for President.'

Now he acted like 26% of the registered voters is actually a mandate. We're all actors in this I suppose.

What has happened is that in the last 20 years America has changed from a producer to a consumer. And all consumers know that when the producer names the tune the consumer has got to dance. That's the way it is. We used to be producers and were very inflexible at that. Now that we are consumers we find things difficult to understand.

Natural resources and minerals will change your world. The Arabs used to be in the Third World. They have bought the Second World and put a firm down payment on the First one. Controlling your resources will control your world.

This country has been surprised by the way the world looks now. They don't know if they want to be diplomats or continue the policy of nuclear nightmare diplomacy. John Foster Dulles ain't nothing but the name of an airport now.

America wants Nostalgia. They want to go back as far as they can, even if it turns out to be only last week. Not to face now or the future, but to face backwards. And yesterday was the time of our cinema heroes riding to the rescue at the last minute; the day of the man on the white horse or the man in the white hat, coming to save America at the last moment. Someone always came to save America at the last moment.

And when America found itself having a hard time facing the future they looked for one of their heroes. Someone like John Wayne. But unfortunately John Wayne was no longer available, so they settled for Ronald the Raygun.

And it has turned into something that we can only look at like a 'B' movie.

PART TWO

'B' MOVIE *THE POEM*

Come with us back to those inglorious days before heroes were zeros. Before fair was square. When the cavalry came straight-away and all-American men were like Hemingway, to the days of the wondrous 'B' movie.

The Producer, underwritten by all the millionaires necessary, will be 'Casper' the defensive Weinburger. No more animated a choice is available.

The director will be 'Attila' the Haig, running around declaring himself 'In charge and in control!' The ultimate realization of inmates taking over at the asylum.

The screenplay will be adapted from the book called *Voodoo Economics* by George 'Papa Doc' Bush.

The theme song will be done by The Village People. That most military tune 'Macho Man'. A theme song for saber rattling and selling wars door-to-door. Remember, we're looking for the closest thing we can find to John Wayne.

Clichés abound like kangaroos courtesy of some spaced out Marlin Perkins, a Raygun contemporary. Clichés like:

'Tall in the saddle.' Like 'Riding on or off into the sunset.' Like 'Qadafi, get off my planet by sunset.' More so than 'He died with his boots on.'

Marine tough, the man is Bogart-tough, Cagney-tough and Hollywood-tough, the man is John Wayne-tough, the man is cheap steak-tough and Bonzo-substantial.

A Madison Avenue masterpiece. A miracle, a cotton candy politician: 'Presto Macho!'

Put your orders in, America, and quick as Kodak we duplicate, with the accent on the dupe!

It's a clear case of selective amnesia: remembering what we want to remember and forgetting what we choose to forget. All of a sudden the man who called for a bloodbath on our college campuses is supposed to be Dudley Goddamn Do-Right?

'You go give them liberals hell, Ronny!' That was the mandate to the new Captain Bligh on the new Ship of Fools.

Obviously based on chameleon performances of the past: as a liberal Democrat. As the head of the Screen Actor's Guild. When other celluloid saviours were cringing in terror from McCarthyism Ron stood tall!

It goes all the way back from Hollywood to Hillbillies, from liberal to libelous, from Bonzo to Birchite to Born Again.

Civil Rights. Gay Rights. Women's Rights. They're all wrong! Call in the cavalry to disrupt this perception of freedom gone wild. First one of them wants freedom and then the whole damn world wants freedom!

Nostalgia. That's what America wants. The good old days. When we 'gave them hell!' When the buck stopped somewhere and you could still buy something with it! To a time when movies were in black and white and so was everything else.

Let us go back to the campaign trail before six-gun Ron shot off his face and developed Hoof in Mouth. Before the free press went down before a full court press and were reluctant to view the menu because they knew that the only meal available was 'crow'.

Lon Chaney, our man of 1,000 faces got nothing on Ron.

Doug Henning will do the makeup.

Special effects by Grecian Formula 16 and Crazy Glue.

Transportation furnished by the David Rockefeller Remote Control Company. Their slogan is: 'Why wait 'til 1984. You can panic now and avoid the rush.'

So much for the good news. As Wall Street goes so goes the nation and here's a look at the closing stocks:

Racism is up. Human Rights are down. Peace is shaky. War items are hot. The House claims all ties. Jobs are down, money is scarce and Common Sense is at an all-time low with heavy trading.

Movies were looking better than ever and now no one is looking because we're all starring in a 'B' movie. And we would have rather had John Wayne. In fact, we would have done better with John Wayne.

PART THREE

RE-RON

Ah yes, they're off and running again. The campaign trail. And doesn't he look like himself? Back in the saddle again.

From Roy Rogers to Buck Rogers to Ginger Rogers to Kenny Rogers to Mr. Rogers to Jolly Rogers. A Re-Ron.

From Gabby Hayes to Rutherford B. Hayes to Helen Hayes to Isaac Hayes to walking around in a bleeping Haze. A Re-Ron.

In the dead of night we've seen it all: Boy George in drag? Or was Maggie Thatcher RayGun in drag?

Maggie and Jiggs. What gigs they got. That's the problem.

It's a Re-Ron. It's Geritol. It's Jerry Mahoney and off the bleeping wall.

He's terrorized and jeopardized and severed ties and sent our spies to plant them mines and told them lies all for the bottom line.

We don't need no Re-Ron.

We don't need no Re-Ron, you know.

We don't need no Re-Ron.

We've seen all the Re-Rons before.

But there he is. Running again. Re-running. Re-ronning. It's a Re-Ron.

A Re-Ron as predicted before the RayGun threats were worldwide inflicted.

All those recent damages and nerve changes. Re-freezing the cold war and lighting a fire under the hot one.

Banging on the war drums and we're listening to the rhythms.

It's a Re-Ron. Milton Berle.

13

The Duke of Wayne. The Duke of Earl.
   Orson Welles doing 'War of the Worlds'.
The Hardy Boys and Georgy Girl.
   It's a Re-Ron. A corruption piece starring
   Raymond Donovan and Edwin Meese.
   It's a Re-Ron. The Latin Plan
and here's our star: Nacho Man!
We don't need no Re-Ron.
We don't need no Re-Ron, you know.
We don't need no Re-Ron.
We've seen all the Re-Rons before.

   It's beyond real-to-reel and Shogun to RayGun.
   And no one has been psyched by cosmetic set changes and
minimal shuffling of the deck of the cast of characters:
   [I was glad to see James Watt go.]
   Secretary of the Inferior. James 'Kilowatt', Kill a Tree, Kill a
Seal!
   Attila The Haig transformed into Peanuts. Called Shultz on
Capitol Hill.
   A dead ringer for the Cowardly Lion from The Wizard of Oz.
And every time I see him I hear the song:
   'We're off to see the Arabs. Off to see the Arabs.'
   Or just off. And up the yellow brick road. Another war
drummer from the Cap Weinburger school of arms pushing
overkill and The Henry Kissinger Peace Academy
We don't need no Re-Ron.
We don't need no Re-Ron, you know.
We don't need no Re-Ron.
We've seen all the Re-Rons before.

And through it all we closed our eyes at 33 and 1/3, didn't we?
Going down for the 3rd time under the 3rd degree.
A 3rd of our fellow Americans breaking their backs for 3rd
    class citizenship,
taking a 3rd less home on payday because of inflation
while 30 years after segregation
was tried, found guilty and banished from the nation
when here it comes again: Discrimination!
And the world watching our response to the 3rd World because
the stakes are the 3rd World War!:
It's the neutron bomb for Lebanon.
He's the gladiator invader of Grenada!
There's millions more for El Salvador!
and he's up to his 'Keisters' with the Sandanistas!
    Would   we   take   Fritz   (Mondale)   without   Grits
(Carter)?
    We'd take Fritz the Cat.
    Would we take Jesse Jackson?
    Hell, we'd take Michael Jackson!
We don't need no Re-Ron.
We don't need no Re-Ron, you know.
We don't need no Re-Ron.
We've seen all the Re-Rons before.

A Re-ron, the late late show.
A black and white flick from ages ago.
A Re-Ron. The late late show.
Ain't we seen this flick somewhere before?

    And then there's stage presence. My, doesn't he look like
himself?

15

A Re-Ron:
The face never changes nor political stance.
He's constantly smiling, a Greek comedy mask.
So cool on the camera. The hair's in place.
The same old lines and the same clichés.
Perfectly rehearsed. Obscuring wrong and right.
He says he's defending some bullshit while he's picking a
    fight.
It's a Re-Ron, a time machine
stuck in reverse and filming new scenes.
20 years gone at the point of a gun.
    To hell with reality: 'Places everyone!'
    It's a Re-Ron. Nostalgia got stoned.
Mom and apple pie.
No place like home.
And leave it to Beaver and the Twilight Zone.
Can't they face it, Goddamnit? Yesterday's gone.

We don't need no Re-Ron.
We don't need no Re-Ron, you know
We don't need no Re-Ron.
We've seen all the Re-Rons before.
A Re-Ron. The late late show. A black and white flick from
    ages ago.
A Re-Ron. The late late show
starring Curly, the RayGun, Larry and Moe.
Like a Saturday morning cartoon show. Like a migraine
    headache you had before.
Cinematic garbaggio.
We don't need no Re-Ron!
We don't need no Re-Ron.

SPACE SHUTTLE

Space was the place
where at least we thought our dreams were safe;
where yesterdays of youth and innocence and grace
floated somewhere high above the planet's face.
Ah, but the distance has been erased
'cause Uncle Sam is on the case.
E.T. is joining the Arms Race!
They're up there building some kinda military base.
Rocketing through the atmosphere,
sliding into second gear
while miles below the people cheer
the New Invaders on the New Frontier.
. . . but there are also those who do not cheer.
The gravity of their lives appears
and in their eyes flash frozen fears
while rocket sounds are all they hear.

Space Shuttle/raising hell down on the ground!
Space Shuttle/turning the seasons upside down.
Space Shuttle/and all the hungry people know
all change sho' 'nuff ain't progress when you're poor.
No matter what man goes looking for
he always seems to find a war.
As soon as dreams of peace are felt
the war is raging somewhere else.

We must have somehow been disarmed
or lost our heads over false alarms;
underwhelmed and over charmed,
watching the storm clouds from afar.
Exploration, proliferation,

spending more while pockets fill.
Assessments of our investments
drive us on to overkill.
Practice looks of great surprise
as the Captain Kirk of 'Free Enterprise'.
Wall Street says 'Let's play Defense!'
and 'Dollar bills make damn good sense!'
Hail to the new Protectionism!
Let's bring on the new age of Humanism.
We can put the cap on Capitalism!
We've got a giant, mechanical Ray-gunism!

Space Shuttle/raising hell down on the ground!
Space Shuttle/turning the seasons upside down.
Space Shuttle/and all the hungry people know
all change sho' 'nuff ain't progress when you're poor.
No matter what man goes looking for
he always seems to find a war.
As soon as dreams of peace are felt
the war is raging somewhere else.

Space was the rage
so Hollyweird took center stage
and together we wondered whether
we would ever get over the weather.
Things started happening that seemed so strange,
like the whole jet stream is being rearranged:
There was a clear day in L.A.,
a foot of snow in Tampa Bay.
The space shuttle no sooner goes up
than we watch while the weather man goes nuts.

Tornados and hurricanes,
dead rivers and Acid Rain,
volcanoes ages dead
suddenly just get up and lose their heads.
Typhoons, monsoons,
and tidal waves come down from an angry moon.
It's earthquaking all the Goddamn time
and the only common denominator we can find . . .
Space Shuttle/raising hell down on the ground!
Space Shuttle/turning the seasons upside down.
Space Shuttle/and all the hungry people know
all change sho' 'nuff ain't progress when you're poor.
No matter what man goes looking for
he always seems to find a war.
As soon as dreams of peace are felt
the war is raging somewhere else.

Old folks must have had it right
from the time they saw the first satellite
they said 'Some advancements may be good,
but not in God's neighborhood.'
Laser beams and moonbeams,
we got peace dreams killed by war schemes,
there's a hole shot through the ozone layer
that has put the fear back into atmos-fear.
ICBM, MX, Cruise Missiles,
obsolete today.
Let's spend another billion on The Sergeant York
and then throw that 'sumbitch' away.
War is big business without a doubt
so there ain't much chance of peace breaking out.

Underwater, overhead, God we'll all be nervous wrecks
'cause did you hear where they're going next?

Space Shuttle/raising hell down on the ground!
Space Shuttle/turning the seasons upside down.
Space shuttle/and all the hungry people know
all change sho' 'nuff ain't progress when you're poor.
No matter what man goes looking for
he always seems to find a war.
As soon as dreams of peace are felt
the war is raging somewhere else.

A rat done bit my sister Nell.
  (with Whitey on the moon)
Her face and arms began to swell.
  (and Whitey's on the moon)
I can't pay no doctor bill.
  (but Whitey's on the moon)
Ten years from now I'll be payin' still.
  (while Whitey's on the moon)
The man jus' upped my rent las' night.
  ('cause Whitey's on the moon)
No hot water, no toilets, no lights.
  (but Whitey's on the moon)
I wonder why he uppin' me?
  ('cause Whitey's on the moon?)
I wuz already payin' 'im fifty a week.
  (with Whitey on the moon)
Taxes takin' my whole damn check,
Junkies make me a nervous wreck,
The price of food is goin' up,
An' as if all that crap wuzn't enough:
A rat done bit my sister Nell.
  (with Whitey on the moon)
Her face an' arm began to swell.
  (but Whitey's on the moon)
Was all that money I made las' year
  (for Whitey on the moon?)
How come there ain't no money here?
(Hmm! Whitey's on the moon)
Y'know I jus' 'bout had my fill
  (of Whitey on the moon.)
I think I'll sen' these doctor bills
  (to Whitey on the moon.)

I was wondering about our yesterdays
and started digging through the rubble
and to tell the truth somebody went
to a hell of a lot of trouble
to make sure that when we looked things up
we wouldn't fare too well
and that we would come up with totally unreliable
pictures of ourselves.
But I've compiled what few facts I could,
I mean, such as they are
to see if I could shed a little bit of light
and this is what I got so far:
First, white folks discovered Africa
and claimed it fair and square.
Cecil Rhodes couldn't have been robbing nobody
'cause he said there was nobody there.
White folks brought all of the civilization
since there wasn't none around.
They said 'How could these folks be civilized
when you never see nobody writing nothing down?'
And to prove all of their suspicions
it didn't take too long.
They found out there were whole groups of people
– *in plain sight* –
running around with no clothes on. That's right!
The women, the men, the young and the old,
righteous white folks covered their eyes.
So no time was spent considering the environment.
Hell no! This here, this just wasn't civilized.
And another way they knew we were backwards,
or at least this is how we were taught,

is that 'Unlike the very civilized people of Europe'
these Black groups actually fought!
And *yes*, they were some 'rather crude implements'
and *yes*, there was 'primitive art'
and *yes*, they were masters of hunting and fishing
and courtesy came from the heart.
And *yes*, there was medicine, love and religion,
inter-tribal communication by drum.
But no papers and pencils and other utensils
and hell, these folks never even heard of a gun.
So this is why the colonies came
to stabilize the land.
Because The Dark Continent had copper and gold
and the discoverers had themselves a plan.
They would 'discover' all the places with promise.
You didn't need no titles or deeds.
You could just appoint people to make everything legal,
to sanction the trickery and greed.
And out in the bushes if the natives got restless
You could call that 'guerilla attack!'
And never have to describe that somebody finally got
wise
and decided they wanted their things back.
But still we are victims of word games,
semantics is always a bitch:
Places once called underdeveloped and 'backwards'
are now called 'mineral rich'.
And still it seems the game goes on
with unity always just out of reach
because Libya and Egypt used to be in Africa,
but they've been moved to the 'Middle East'.

There are examples galore I assure you,
but if interpreting was left up to me
I'd be sure every time folks knew this version wasn't mine
which is why it is called 'His story'.

DR. KING (from *The Last Holiday*)

The Artist had honestly never given much thought
As to how much of a battle would have to be fought
To get most Americans to agree and to say
That there actually should be a black holiday.
But what a hell of a challenge. How far was Stevie willing to
go
To make them pass an amendment left on the table 10 years
in a row?
The Artist never doubted that Stevie was sincere
But how many minds had come together in the last 12 years?
How many folks recognised how much America had to grow?
And who else had been qualified to lead us where we had to go?
The Artist had liked the idea of a minister being around
When racing for high stakes, to have his foot near the brakes
Because of what truly could have gone down.
Because America could have blown up
Before it ever could be said that we had grown up.

Ghandi took non-violence with him when he died
Over here there was non-violence but only on one side.
When white folks beat up on and killed people that you knew
You decided to direct your anger at a building or two.
Instead of making the Old Testament a Civil Rights guide
And saying that 'an eye for an eye' would now be justified
We were told to accept that some white folks had no class
And as opposed to condemning all the white folks 'en masse'.
We determined that remaining peaceful was the best thing.
And directing those feeling were men like Dr. King.
Through a storm of provocation to fight we saw
That in order to change America you must change the law.
We were called 'militant' and 'radical' and made to look bad

For trying to secure the rights all Americans had.
But between what's written and what's done is the real thing
So America might not have made it without Dr. Martin
Luther King.

A TOAST TO THE PEOPLE

And though its been too long and
Too many years have passed
And though the time has gone,
The memories still hold fast.

Yes, as strange as it seems
We still live in the past.
The essence of a Black life
Lost in the hour-glass.

And ever since we came to this land
This country has rued the day
When we would stand as one
And raise our voices and say:

You know there won't be no more killings
And no more talk of class;
Your sons and your daughters
Won't die in the hour-glass.

A toast to David Walker
A toast to Martin King
A toast to all the leaders who had a golden dream.
A toast to all Black fathers who lived their lives in vain.
A toast to all Black mothers who shouldered this life in pain.

A toast to the people.

The world!
Planet Earth; third from the Sun of a gun, 360 degrees.
And as new worlds emerge
stay alert. Stay aware.
Watch the Eagle! Watch the Bear!
Earthquaking, foundation shaking,
bias breaking, new day making change.
Accumulating, liberating, educating, stimulating change!
Tomorrow was born yesterday.
From inside the rib or people cage
the era of our first blood stage was blotted or erased
or TV screened or defaced.
Remember there's a revolution going on in the world.
One blood of the early morning
revolves to the one idea of our tomorrow.
Homeboy, hold on!
Now more than ever all the family must come together.
Ideas of freedom and harmony, great civilizations
yesterday brought today will bring tomorrow.
We must be about
earthquaking, liberating, investigating
and new day making change in
the world.

WORK FOR PEACE[1]

Introduction:
Back when Eisenhower was the President
Golf courses was where most of his time was spent.
So I never paid much attention to what the President said
Because in general, I believed the General was politically dead,
But he always seemed to know how muscles were going to be
                                                        flexed
He kept mumbling something about a military-industrial complex.

The military and monetary
The military and monetary
The military and monetary

The military and the monetary
Get together whenever they think its necessary
They have turned our brothers and sisters into mercenaries,
They are turning the planet into a cemetery.

The military and the monetary
Use the media as intermediaries.
They are determined to keep the citizens secondary
They make so many decisions that seem arbitrary.

We've been standing behind the 'Commander-in-Chief'
Who was under a spotlight, shaking like a leaf
Because the ship of state had landed on an economic reef
So we knew he'd be bringing us messages of grief.

The military and monetary
Were 'Shielded'[2] by January and went 'Storming'[3] into February.
They brought us pot-bellied Generals as luminaries.
Two weeks before I hadn't heard of the sons of Bitches
And then all of a sudden they were legendary.

29

They took the honor from the honorary
They took the dignity from the dignitaries
They took the secrets from the secretaries
But they left the 'bitch' in 'obituary'

Yeah, they had some 'smart bombs'
But they had some dumb ones as well
They scared the hell outta CNN in that Baghdad hotel.

The military and the monetary
The military and monetary
The military and monetary

Get together whenever they think its necessary
War in the desert sometimes sure could seem scary
But they beamed out the war to all of their subsidiaries
Tried making 'so damn insane' (Saddam Hussein) a worthy
                                            adversary
Keeping all of the citizens secondary
Scaring old folks into coronaries
Making us all wonder if all of this was really, truly necessary.

We've got to *work* for peace.
We've got to work for peace.
If we all believed in peace we could have peace.
The only thing wrong with peace is that
You can't make no money from it.

The military and the monetary
Get together whenever they think it's necessary
They have turned our brothers and sisters into mercenaries
We are turning parts of the planet into a cemetery.

We hounded the Ayatollah religiously,
Bombed Libya and killed Qadafi's son hideously.
We turned our back on our allies, the Panamanians
Watched Ollie North selling guns to the Iranians
Witnessed Gorbachev slaughtering Lithuanians
So we better warn the Amish, they may bomb the
Pennsylvanians.

We've got to work for peace.
Peace ain't coming this way.
We've got to work for peace.

Peace is not (merely) the absence of war
It is the absence of the rumors of war and the threats of war
And the preparation for war.
Peace is not (merely) the absence of war
We will have all touched the power of peace within ourselves.
Because we will have all come to peace within ourselves.

Peace ain't gonna be easy.
Peace ain't gonna be free.
We've got to work for peace.

(*SPIRITS* 1994 TVT RECORDS)

FOOTNOTES:
1. The poem is also known as 'The Military and the Monetary' and also
'So Damn Insane'
2. The 'Gulf War' January phase was coded 'Desert Shield'
3. The 'Gulf War' February phase was coded 'Desert Storm'

WHAT YOU SEE AIN'T WHAT YOU GOETZ

I get the sho' 'nuff blues
checkin' out the *Daily News*
no matter which way it's comin' from
I'm told I'm not supposed to choose
just accept the newsman's views
but that sho' ain't no happy medium

You see all I want is the facts
but blow-dried hairdos is gettin' into the act
because reporters are expert observers
they establish social trends
decidin' who's out and who's in
and rush in with the tragedies that unnerve us

Syndicated columnists
lookin' to get their asses kissed
cause they're the big shots of political affairs
and the anchorman's job
is to look extra suave
while they're trying to convince us that they care

The radio commentator
is a five minute narrator
whose news is perpetually grim
and his ego is blown
he's got a great baritone
but the cameras ain't never on him

But the message is clear
they want all Black folks to hear
that the price you got to pay to be free

you get told how to feel
you get told what is real
to be exactly how they want you to be

you get the rational logical
sound philosophical
poetic distortions
political contortions
cause white folks still ain't ready yet
so what you hear ain't gonna be what you get

Now some folks may call me a radical
or remind me that at best I'm not practical
to keep pointing out what everyone should know
but we're still looking for justice
while other folks devise ways to bust us
so we spend more time in court than McEnroe

Because when the time for freedom came
folks started feeling only the surface had changed
instead of celebrating 'Free at last!'
'Cause all the racists had said 'Okay'
because equality can work both ways
and they promptly started kicking poor white folk's ass

How can the issue be race
when every citizen can take his or her case
and be heard by a jury of their peers?
meanwhile I'm listening to the rundown
about four young brothers who was gunned down
by some psycho with imaginary fears

When you get down to the real nitty-gritty
you're on a subway in New York City
and Bernhard, the gunman, shows upon the set
and he decides these four young Blacks
are about to launch an attack
though they hadn't attacked nobody yet

Regardless, Bernie makes his play
and he's like Eastwood saying 'Make my fuckin' day!' and
in self-defense he even shoots someone wounded on the floor.
then he confesses on video tape,
but since he was in an 'agitated state'
he's acquitted and let out to shoot some more

Now does this mean every sister and brother
Mexican, Indian, Oriental or other
won't ever see homicide put them behind bars?
Because it legitimately terrifies me
to know that the next sumbitch I see
might be armed and just as crazy as Bernhard

Or is this proof that the system works
or are we all being treated like jerks?
Take your chance and step right up to place your bets
and I'm gonna put my money down
saying if it's ever the other way around
we'll find out that what you see ain't what you Goetz

THOUGHT OUT

we just thought it was a drink,
but maybe had there been more time to think . . .
a cognac on the rocks and a glass of white wine
crowd thinning out cause it's near closing time
laughs, cigarette smoke, an adult's playroom
where foreplay for players who like adult freedom
and dimly dark lowlight sparks . . .
we just thought it was different
like a pleasant surprise
and maybe we wouldn't have said so much as 'hello'
had we looked around into other folks' eyes
we just thought it was cool
but not the rigid, frigid,
frozen, not-chosen
petrified, paralyzed
ossified ostracized
put out to pasture is the ultimate disaster
we just thought it was a glance
almost something thought to yourself
a second look, a double give and take
a 'very nice, my lady' and/or
an appraisal of the up-closer, 'hmm'
we thought it was a change of pace
an hour away, a quiet someplace
just to talk, walk, speak, peek
see behind that sudden jolt,
an electric unexpected volts
probably nothing but might be fun
if not, nobody lost nobody won
but much more suddenly than all at once,
an unexpected cloud that blocks the sun

and before we heard the starter's gun
too soon to know it was too late to run
we thought it was no big deal
we thought it had an ugly feel
a curious, furious over reaction
that there would be no end to the distractions
unless we gave up
and said we'd had enough
and we had thought it was ours.

My life is one of movement
I been running as fast as I can
I've inherited trial and error directly from my old man
But I'm committed to the consequences
Whether I stand or fall
And when I get back to my life
I think I'm gonna give her a call

She's been waiting patiently
For me to get myself together
And it touched something deep inside
When she said she'd wait forever
Because forever's right up on me now
That is, if it ever comes at all
And when I get back to my life
I think I'm gonna give her a call

She didn't know, she could hardly believe
How much she means to me
She wouldn't know, she could scarcely understand
Why I cling so desperately to dreams
'Cause she's calmed me in the evening
She's calmed me in the night
She's calmed my fear of dreaming
And maybe my fear of life
My life's been one of running away
Just as fast as I can
But I've been no more successful at getting away
Than was my old man
But if you come to recognize the truth
And understand that the truth is really all
That when I get back to my life
I think I'm gonna give her a call

To say any words you ain't feeling
Don't seem to be what she needs
She's been hurt a lot and put down a lot
But she don't really need your sympathy
'Cause her touch is soft and her eyes are smiling
Though small-time people try and put her down.
She ain't done nobody wrong
The love she has is gonna keep her strong
(It seems like) long after love has abandoned you and me
You might see her running to work in the morning
Remember there's a whole lot on her mind
If you've got nothing to say
Why not let her go on her way
'Cause brother, everybody just ain't got the time

THE 'GOLDFINGER' AFFAIR

The artist lucked into a couple of good seats
And told a girl he'd walked around with for a week.
And when she spoke up saying that she'd like to go
It was like being nominated for his own double-O.
Because no exaggeration let's just say she was 'impressive'
And taking her out would be considered thoroughly
'progressive'.

She needed someone who knew karate
And called a 'Scott' from Scotland Yard.
And if you were into guarding bodies
She had a body you would love to guard.
Keep all the freaks and creeps out of her hair.
A holiday weekend knight in the middle of Times Square
And he put the 'lean' inside of 'clean'
And took the 'cool' letters out of 'school'
And the last thing that he would ever dream
Was being set up and treated like a fool.
No! 'Set up' implies conspiracy,
A deliberately crooked deal
But you didn't need X-ray vision to see
That her family's shock was real.
No they weren't surprised that he was black
Or forgotten that they were white
This wasn't a formal marriage proposal
So that wasn't the issue that night.
The doorman walked him **through** the lobby to the back
But he was too fuckin' excited to even notice that
But riding up the shaft, it smelled a bit ripe in the elevator
Floor slippery, a helluva draft, that all came to him later.
The pulleys was whining and bitching
The whole box was bumping and pitching

39

He was about to ask the pilot about ditching
When the door opened and he was standing in the kitchen
The family 'recovered' it up like it happened all the time
The smiles were so bright the Artist damn near went blind
His face was on fire and he was relieved to be a brother
His red-faced embarrassment couldn't be 'read' by the others.

He was stammering as he met the adults
His heart was hammering as he examined the doorman's
                                                    insult
He feels like he's made of plaster frozen there before- hand
He conceals that his mind is on the bastard, the
                                    motherfuckin' doorman,
He pictures the broad-shouldered man, his tacky uniform
                                                    sagging
Inside the basement cave with the maintenance crew
This sonofabitch is bragging
**'Some nigger,' he spits. 'Goin' upstairs to date her
So I take him up there** *in the service elevator!*
The janitor and the elevator man laughed till they cry
Thinking about how their colleague just embarrassed some
                                                    guy.

The Artist wanted to explain that their plans for the night
Were no longer in effect
He wanted to complain that he wasn't feeling right
And had a terrible pain in the neck
Apologize quickly and not linger
Advise them to **'Call 9–1–1 fast',**
Leave them the tickets, they could go to 'Goldfinger'
He would go back downstairs to kick some ass!

40

Yeah! For two years he had hung out with the preps
But he came from **'little San Juan'**
And down there he'd once had a pretty decent rep
And an insult justified 'gettin' it on'.

But doesn't it happen like that all the time
Brothers ending up on their way to the joint
If they don't damage your body they fuck with your mind
And you never reach no terminal point
It's not the one insult.
It's not the word 'nigger!'
And each day is a little more difficult
Holding back the rage leaves you terribly bitter
And this was one the Artist managed to resist
Flexing his fingers, not letting them roll up into a fist
Because that would have hurt his Mom and everybody else
So he took the girl to James Bond and was humiliated by
    himself.

. . . because i always feel like running.
not away,
. . . because there's no such place.
. . . because if there was
i would have found it by now
. . . because it's easier to run; easier than staying
and finding out you're the only one who didn't run
. . . because running will be the way your life and mine
will be described:
as in the long run or
as in having given someone a run for his money or
as in running out of time
. . . because running makes me look like everyone else
though i hope there will never
be cause for that
. . . because i will be running in the other direction:
not running for cover;
. . . because if i knew where cover was
i would stay there and never have to run for it.
not running for my life
. . . because i have to be running
for something of more value to be running
and not in fear;
. . . because the thing i fear cannot be
escaped, eluded, avoided,
hidden from, protected from, gotten away from,
not without showing the fear
as i see it now
. . . because closer, clearer/no sir nearer
. . . because of you, and
. . . because of the nice that you

quietly, quickly be causing and
. . . because you're going to see me run soon, and
. . . because you're going to know why i'm running.
then.
you'll know then
. . . because i'm not going to tell you now.

IS THAT JAZZ?

Basie was never really commonplace
He was always measures ahead.
Ellington was more than number one
For the music and things that he said.
Bird was the word back when tenors were heard
From Kansas right up to *the Prez*
And *Billie* was really the Queen of a scene
That keeps echoing on in my head.

What it has will surely last but is that Jazz?

Miles had a style that amazes and raises
The spirits from deep in your soul.
'Trane struck a vein of laughter and pain
Adventures the mind could explore.
Stevie and *Bob* talk of freedom and 'jam'
In their own individual ways.
Playing and singing as long as its bringing
A message in all that it says.

What it has will surely last but is that Jazz?

We overanalyse we let others define
A thousand precious feelings from our past.
When we express love and tenderness
Is that Jazz? Is that Jazz? Is that Jazz? *Is that Jazz?*

Dizzy's been busy while *Grover* gets us over
With notes that go straight to the heart.
Brother *Ron* gets it on with a baseline so strong
That the sounds seem to grow in the dark.

I take pride in what's mine – is that really a crime –
When you know I ain't got nothing else?
Only millions of sounds pick me up when I'm down;
Let me salvage a piece of myself.

What it has will surely last but is that Jazz?

LADY DAY AND JOHN COLTRANE

Ever feel kinda down and out and don't know
    just what to do?
Livin' alla your days in darkness, let the sun shine
    through.
Ever feel that somehow, somewhere you lost
    your way?
And if you don't get help you won't make it
    through the day.
You could call on Lady Day!
You could call on John Coltrane!
They'll wash your troubles, your troubles away.

Plastic people with plastic minds on their way to
    plastic homes.
There's no beginning, there ain't no ending
just on and on and on and on and . . .
It's all because we're so afraid to say that we're
    alone
until our hero rides in, rides in on his
    saxophone.
You could call on Lady Day!
You could call on John Coltrane!
They'll wash your troubles, your troubles away.

Free will is free mind. Free to evaluate the systems that control our lives from without and free to examine the emotions that control our perspective from within.

Black people everywhere are becoming aware of the gaps that exist between the 'American' values and the values of our spirits. The nature of our spirits demand a lifestyle apart from the American life speed – a lifestyle that accents life and not death, love and not hate.

We have things to do for tomorrow. Our children will have to deal with all the mistakes we make today. To live in dignity they will have to erase many of the peronsal compromises we made. We must actively search out the truth and help each other.

We do not need more legislation or more liberals. What we need is self-love and self-respect. By every means necessary!

Unfortunately, it is not easy to lvoe yourself after you heard hatred and self-destruction in every city. We must make the extra effort needed to identify the true enemies of our peace of mind.

We can begin by realizing that though we are trapped by economic and geographical boundaries. we are still capable of spiritual freedom supported by the truth.

What we do with the truth is the key to our freedom.

Notes from *Reflection on Free Will* (15/5/72)
'. . . words are important for the mind/notes are for the soul.'
(from 'Plastic Pattern People,' 11/67)

glad to get high and see the slow motion world,
just to reach and touch the half-notes floating.
world spinning quicker than 9/8 Dave Brubeck. we
   come now frantically searching for Thomas
   More rainbow villages.
    up on suddenly Charlie Mingus and Ahmed
     Abdul-Malik
to add bass to a bottomless pit of insecurity. you
   may be plastic because
you never meditate about the bottom of glasses,
the third side of your universe.
       add on
Alice Coltrane and her cosmic strains, still no
   vocal
on blue-black horizons your plasticity is tested
by a formless assault: THE SUN can answer
   questions
in tune to sacrificial silence but why will our
new jazz age give us no more expanding puzzles?
   (Enter John) blow from under always and
     never so that,
the morning may shout of brain-
bending saxophones.
   the third world arrives with Yusef Lateef
and
Pharoah Sanders with oboes straining to touch the
core of your unknown soul.
   Ravi Shankar comes
   with strings attached/prepared to stabilize
   your seventh sense (Black Rhythm!)
up and down a silly ladder run the notes without

the words. words are important for the mind/the
notes are for the soul.
       Miles Davis? SO WHAT?
     Cannonball, Fiddler, Mercy
    Dexter Gordon, ONE flight UP
  Donald Byrd, Cristo
        but what about words?
would you like to survive on sadness/call on
  Ella and Jose Happiness
      drift with
Smoky, Bill Medley, Bobby Taylor
Otis/soul music where frustrations are
washed by drums – come Nina and Miriam –
congo/mongo beat me senseless
bongo/tonto – flash through dream worlds of
  STP and LSD. SpEeD kilLs and
sometimes
music's call to the Black is confused. our
speed is our life pace/not safe/not good.
i beg you to escape
  and live
    and hear all of the real. to survive in a
      sincere second of self-self
until a call comes for you to cry elsewhere.
     we
  must all cry, but must the tears be white?

It should be pointed out, I believe, that there are specific individuals or works of art from individual artists that are the source of creative ideas. As such the efforts that are inspired in that direction become *extensions* or *complements*. (At least the succeeding artist hopes that his work is a compliment.)

'Spirits':
'Spirits' was inspired by the John Coltrane composition 'Equinox'. It signified September 23rd, the midway point in the yearly cycle, 180 days from March 20th, recognized in some places as New Year's Day. September 23rd, the beginning of Libra, the beginning of Autumn, is the yearly point where the sun is directly over the equator and day and night are exactly twelve hours long. (Performed on *Spirits.*)

'Inner City Blues':
Inspired by the Marvin Gaye song 'Inner City Blues' and is a compliment/supplement to what I consider to be a tune that still carries a great deal of relevance. (Performed on *Reflections.*)

'Cane':
Inspired by the Jean Toomer book written during the Harlem Renaissance. The first two characters examined are 'Karintha' and 'Becky', two incredibly well-drawn women that I was touched by and wanted to expand people's awareness of. (Performed on *Secrets.*)

'We Almost Lost Detroit':
Comes from the book by John Fuller that examined an accident at the Enrico Fermi nuclear power plant outside of Detroit in 1967. (Performed on *Bridges.*)

SPIRITS

The world spins around us
We search for a balance
The secrets lie in darkness and light
Our lives are like treasures
Unveiled as perfection
A gift to us from spirits on high
Equator. Divider. Equate us. Combine us.
To seek the answers beyond our sight . . .

So you say you never heard of the 'Inner City Blues'
And what's more you don't understand it all
What the ghetto folks mean about 'living behind walls'?
Then put on your best suit, white shirt and tie
And come on downtown to stand in line
For a job washing dishes but you may not qualify.
Walking a great big hole in a new pair of shoes
And you've had your first look at the 'Inner City Blues'.

Go looking for a place to live but all the while
Beware of what's lurking behind the devil's smile.
Are we stupid or just naive that we continue to believe
Money can buy us anything
Including a slice of 'the American Dream'?
Answer ads in the paper about 'houses for sale'
And get treated like Charles Manson out on bail
When you start to get frustrated by the tactics they use
You can recognize that, it's the 'Inner City Blues'.
It makes you wanna holler and throw up both your hands.

And haven't you ever wondered about
Why some brothers and sisters were down and out?
Receiving their sympathy from a bottle of wine
Or worse yet 'old homicide'
Living their lives in a glassine bag
While praising the mysteries of terminal scag?
Still other brothers are parading in drag?
Another set of victims too whipped to choose
You can recognize that its the 'Inner City Blues'
It makes you wanna holler and throw up both your hands!

To see sweet sisters, the blossoms of our African tree
Profiling on the corners talking about 'ten and three'
Because in spite of all the money we made and taxes we paid
The woman was looking at hungry babes
And some decisions had to be made
Could you tell her it's better to go to your grave
As a slave to the minimum wage.
Well I hardly think so but
It makes you wanna holler sometimes and throw up both
   your hands.

And what happens when people decide
That they have nothing to lose?
Did you ever hear about Mark Essex
And the things that made him choose
To fight the 'Inner City Blues'?
Yeah! Essex took to the rooftops guerrilla-style
And watched as all the crackers went wild.
Brought in 600 troops, I hear
Brand new to see them crushed by fear
Essex fought back with a thousand rounds
And New Orleans was a changing town
And rat-a-tat, tat-tat-tat, was the only sound.
Bring on the stoner rifles to knock down walls!
Bring on the god damn elephant guns!
Bring on the helicopters to block out the sun!
Made the devil wanna holler
Because eight were dead and a dozen was down
And cries for freedom were the only sounds
New York, Chicago, 'Frisco, L.A.
Justice was served and the unjust were afraid

Because after all the years and all the fears
Brothers were alive to courage found
And spreading those god damn blues around!
Yeah! makes you wanna holler black people
And hold up both your hands and say 'Liberation'

This poem was recorded on 'Reflections' (1981, Arista).
First performed as a part of a medley between the songs
'Essex' by Bilal Sunni-Ali (recorded on the 1975 Arista LP
South Africa to South Carolina) *and 'Inner City Blues' by*
Marvin Gaye (recorded on the 1971, Motown LP What's Going
On.

Take Karintha
Take Karintha
(As) perfect as dusk when the sun goes down
Take Karintha
(As) perfect as twilight as a child
  Able to drive both young and old wild
(As) perfect as dusk when the sun goes down
And remember, remember every sound
'Cause often as our flowers bloom
Men will try and cut them down
Take Karintha
  She's as sweet as spring rain
  And run from the cane
  Run from the cane

Pray for Becky
Pray for Becky
  White woman gave
Birth to two Black sons
Pray for Becky
  Her one room shack fell to the ground
The two boys killed a man
  And had to leave town
  White woman gave
    Birth to two Black sons
And remember, remember the days
She looked to us for help
And we all turned away
Pray for Becky
Buried down near the trains
    Deep in the cane
    Deep in the cane

WE ALMOST LOST DETROIT

It stands out on the highway
Like a creature from another time
It inspires the baby's question ('Mama, what's that?')
They ask their mothers as they ride.
But no one stops to think about the babies
Or how they would survive
And we almost lost Detroit this time
How would we ever get over losing our minds?

Just 30 miles from Detroit
Stands a giant power station
That ticks each night as the city sleeps
Just seconds from annihilation
But no one stops to think about the people
On how they would survive
And we almost lost Detroit this time
How would we ever get over losing our minds?

The Sheriff of Monroe County
Had (sho' 'nuff) disasters on his mind
And what would Karen Silkwood say to you
If she was still alive?
That when it comes to people's safety
Money wins out every time
And we almost lost Detroit this time
How would we ever get over losing our minds?

I THINK I'LL CALL IT MORNING

I'm gonna take myself a piece of sunshine
and paint it all over my sky.
Be no rain. Be no rain.
I'm gonna take the song from every bird
and make them sing it just for me.
Be no rain.
And I think I'll call it morning from now on.
Why should I survive on sadness
convince myself I've got to be alone?
Why should I subscribe to this world's
    madness
knowing that I've got to live on?

I think I'll call it morning from now on.
I'm gonna take myself a piece of sunshine
and paint it all over my sky.
Be no rain. Be no rain.
I'm gonna take the song from every bird
and make them sing it just for me.
Why should I hang my head?
Why should I let tears fall from my eyes
when I've seen everything that there is to see
and I know that there ain't no sense in crying!
    I know that there ain't no sense in crying!
I think I'll call it morning from now on.

On a bright spring morning
Not a cloud in the sky;
Got me out here walkin', wavin' to the ladies
As they stroll by.
And I ain't forgot for a moment
All the things I need to do,
But when I see that old sun shinin'
It makes me think that I can make it too.
All I really want to say
Is that problems come and go
But the sunshine seems to stay.
Just look around, I think we've found
A lovely day.

Flowers woke up bloomin',
Put on a color show just for me.
Shadows dark and gloomy
I tell them all to stay the hell away from me.
Because I don't feel like believin'
Everything I do got to turn out wrong
When vibrations I'm receivin'
Say hold on brother! Just you be strong.
All I really want to say
Is that problems come and go
But the sunshine remains.

Just look around, I think we've found
A lovely day.

Sometimes it rains and I feel kind of strange.
Because it seems that my problems begin
Without the sunshine on which I depend.

BEGINNINGS (The First Minute of a New Day)

We're sliding through completely new
beginnings.
We're searching out our every doubt
and winning.
We want to be free
and yet we have no idea
why we are struggling here
faced with our every fear
just to survive.

We've heard the sound and come around
to listening.
We've touched the vibes time after time
insisting that we know what life means;
still we can't break away
from dues we've got to pay
we hope will somehow say
that we're alive.

NO KNOCK (*to be slipped into John Mitchell's Suggestion Box*)

You explained it to me John I must admit,
but just for the record you was talkin' shit!
Long raps about No Knock being legislated
for the people you've always hated
in this hell-hole that you/we all call 'home'.
'No Knock!' The Man will say, 'to keep that man
   from beatin' his wife!'
'No Knock!' The Man will say, 'to keep people
   from hurtin' themselves!'
No-Knockin', head rockin', enter shockin',
   shootin', cussin',
killin', cryin', lyin' and bein' white!
No Knocked on my brother, Fred Hampton,
bullet holes all over the place!
No knocked on my brother, Michael Harris
and jammed a shotgun against his skull!
For my protection?
Who's gonna protect me from you?
The likes of you? The nerve of you!
To talk that shit face-to-face
your tomato face dead pan
your dead pan deadening another freedom plan!
No Knockin', head rockin', enter shockin',
   shootin', cussin',
killin', cryin', lyin' and bein' white!
But if you're wise, No Knocker,
you'll tell your No-Knockin' lackies
to No Knock on my brother's heads
and No Knock on my sister's heads
and double lock your door
because soon someone may be No Knocking . . .
   for you!

BILLY GREEN IS DEAD

'The economy's in an uproar,
the whole damn country's in the red,
taxi fares is goin' up . . . What?
You say Billy Green is dead?'
'The government can't decide on busin'
Or at least that's what they said.
Yeah, I heard when you tol' me,
You said Billy Green is dead.'
'But let me tell you 'bout these hotpants
that this big-legged sista wore
when I partied with the frat boys.
You say Billy took an overdose?'
'Well now, junkies will be junkies,
But did you see Gunsmoke las' night?
Man they had themselves a shootout
an' folks wuz dyin' left and right!
At the end when Matt was cornered
I had damn near give up hope . . .
Why you keep on interruptin' me?
You say my son is takin' dope?
Call a lawyer! Call a doctor!
What you mean I shouldn't scream?
My only son is on narcotics,
should I stand here like I'm pleased?'
Is that familiar anybody?
Check out what's inside your head,
because it never seems to matter
when it's Billy Green who's dead.

From the Indians who welcomed the pilgrims
to the buffalo who once ruled the plains;
like the vultures circling beneath the dark clouds
looking for the rain, looking for the rain.
From the cities that stagger on the coast lines
in a nation that just can't take much more
like the forest buried beneath the highways
never had a chance to grow, never had a chance
    to grow.
It's winter; winter in america
and all of the healers have been killed or forced
    away.
It's winter; winter in america
and ain't nobody fighting 'cause nobody knows
    what to save.
The con-stitution was a noble piece of paper;
with Free Society they struggled but they died in
    vain
and now Democracy is ragtime on the corner
hoping that it rains, hoping that it rains.
And I've seen the robins perched in barren
    treetops
watching last ditch racists marching across the
    floor
and like the peace signs that melted in our
    dreams
never had a chance to grow, never had a
    chance to grow.
It's winter; winter in america
and all of the healers done been killed or put in
    jail

it's winter, winter in america
and ain't nobody fighting 'cause nobody knows
  what to save.

Winter is a metaphor – a term used not only to describe the season of ice, but this period of our lives through which we are traveling.

In our hearts we feel that Spring is just around the corner; a Spring of brotherhood and united spirits among people of color. Everyone is moving, searching. There is a restlessness within our souls that keeps us questioning, discovering, struggling against a system that will not allow us space and time for fresh expression. Western Icemen have attempted to distort time.

We approach Winter, the most depressing period in the history of his Western Empire, with threats of oil shortages and energy crises. But we, as Black people, have been a source of endless energy, endless beauty and endless determination. I have many things to tell you about tomorrow's love and light. We will see you in the Spring.

In the interest of national security, please help us carry out our constitutional duty to overthrow the king.

Notes from *Winter In America* (10/73)

THE BOTTLE

See that Black boy over there, runnin' scared
his ol' man's in a bottle.
He done quit his 9 to 5 to drink full time
so now he's livin' in the bottle.
See that Black boy over there, runnin' scared
his 'ol man got a problem.
Pawned off damn near everything, his ol'
   woman's weddin' ring for a bottle.
And don't you think it's a crime
when time after time, people in the bottle.

See that sista, sho' wuz fine before she
started drinkin' wine
from the bottle.
Said her ol' man committed a crime
and he's doin' time,
so now she's in the bottle.
She's out there on the avenue, all by herself
sho' needs help from the bottle.
Preacherman tried to help her out,
she cussed him out and hit him in the head with a bottle.
And don't you think it's a crime
when time after time, people in the bottle.

See that gent in the wrinkled suit
he done damn near blown his cool
to the bottle.
He wuz a doctor helpin' young girls along
if they wuzn't too far gone to have problems.
But defenders of the dollar eagle
Said 'What you doin', Doc, it ain't legal,'

and now he's in the bottle.
Now we watch him everyday tryin' to
chase the pigeons away
from the bottle.
And don't you think it's a crime
when time after time, people in the bottle.

WHEN YOUR GIRLFRIEND HAS A BETTER FRIEND

Let me give you something straight up my friend
Your whole life can turn super funky
And put a too large foot in your rear end
If you're digging a dame who's a junky.

I'm sure I don't need to take you back down the road
And retell all the details about smack
But believe me it's still out there breaking the codes
And its ten times worse than cheeba or crack.

And 'Fuck! How in the world did we come to be friendly?'
And all them other bullshit clichés
And you don't know what you'da done if you'da been me
Just be glad that there wasn't no fuckin way.

Okay then, just for a minute let's both speculate
And since you would be me, I would be you
So now as you (I) can get puffed up and be real fuckin great
About what I (meaning you) should or shouldn't do.

I can hear it all now knowing just what you'd say
About not hangin' out in the streets
And immediately we know there ain't no f'n way
'Cause if it wasn't no hangin' out it wasn't me.
This is gonna sound weak and it ain't no excuse
But it's been years since I'd been around scag
And acting self-righteous is the quickest way to lose
And to tell you the truth it's a drag.

Remembering the shivers and quivers and shakes
Starts to bring the butterflies back to your gut
But junkies don't care what you think are mistakes
She says 'Are you givin' up the money or what?'

You can climb in the pulpit for a sermon or two
Keep your money and watch while she packs
But you know more than precisely what she's gonna do
Go for twenty somewhere lying on her back

Or end up in an alley trying to turn a quick trick
Pushers don't care how the money is made
And when the addict starts getting uptight for a fix
They say 'Fuck gonorrhea and fuck A.I.D.S!'

In the end it ain't theories or jive-ass philosophy
Or what the papers or politicians think
And nobody needs no more heroin (methadone) sociology
While the speaker pours himself another drink.

So you're right. Congratulations on what was weak about
    me
I admit I look like somebody's flunky
But right ain't always the best thing to be
When the girl that you love is a junky.

Jagged jigsaw pieces
Tossed about the room
I saw my Grandma sweeping
With her old straw broom
But she didn't know what she was doing
She could hardly understand
coz she was really sweeping up
Pieces of a Man.
I saw my Daddy meet the Mailman
And I heard the Mailman say
'Now don't you take this letter too hard now, Jimmy,
coz they've laid off nine others today.'
But he didn't know what he was saying
He could hardly understand
That he was only talking to
Pieces of a Man.
I saw the thunder and heard the lightning
And felt the burden of his shame
And for some unknown reason
He never turned my way
Pieces of that letter
Were tossed about the room
And now I hear the sound of sirens
Come knifing through the gloom
But they don't know what they are doing
They could hardly understand
That they're only arresting . . .
Pieces of a Man.
I saw him go to pieces
He was always such a good man
He was always such a strong, strong man!
Yeah, I saw him go to pieces

I saw him go to pieces
. . . *mid-winter*
There is a revolution going on in America/the
World; a shifting in the winds/vibrations, as disruptive
as an actual earth-tremor, but it is happening in
our hearts.

There is a revolution going on in America/the
World; a change as swift as blackening skies when
the rains come, as fresh and clear as the air after the
rain. We need change.

The seeds of this revolution were planted hundreds
of years ago; in slave ships, in cotton fields, in
tepees, in the souls of brave men. The seeds were
watered, nurtured and bloom now in our hands as
we rock our babies.

It is mid-winter in America; a man-made season of
shattered dreams and shocked citizens, fumbling
and frustrated beneath the crush of greed of
corporate monsters and economic manipulators
gone wild. There are bitter winds born in the
knowledge of secret plans hatched by Western
Money Men that backfired and grew out of control
to eat its own.

We must support ourselves and stand fast
together even as pressure disperses our enemies
and bangs at our doors. No one can do everything,
but everybody can do something. We must all do
what we can for each other to weather this blizzard.
Now more than ever all the family must be
together; to comfort, to protect, to guide, to survive
because . . . there is a revolution going on in
America/the World.
Notes from *First Minute of a New Day* (1/75)

SMALL TALK AT 125TH AND LENOX

Tell me:

Did'ja ever eat corn bread an' black-eyed peas?
Or watermelon and mustard greens?
Get high as you can on Saturday night
and then go to church on Sunday to set things
right?

Listen:

'I seen Miz Blake after Willie yesterday.
She'd a killed anybody who'd a got in her way!
Hey look! I got a tv for a pound on the head.
Jimmy Gene got the bes' Panamanian Red.
No, I ain't got on no underclothes,
But the Hawk got to get through this Gypsy Rose!
I think Clay got his very good points.
You say a trey bag wit' thirteen joints?
Who cares if LBJ is in town?
Up with Stokely an' H. Rap Brown!
I dunno if the riots is wrong,
But Whitey been kickin' my ass fo' too long.
I wuz s'pose to baby but they hel' my pay.
Did you hear what the number wuz yesterday?
Junkies is all right when they ain't broke.
They leaves you alone when they high on dope.
Damn, but I wish I could get up an' move!
Shut up, hell, you know that ain't true.'

Picture a man of nearly thirty
who seems twice as old with clothes torn and
    dirty.
Give him a job shining shoes
or cleaning out toilets with bus station crews.
Give him six children with nothing to eat.
Expose them to life on a ghetto street.
Tie an old rag around his wife's head and
have her pregnant and lying in bed.
Stuff them all in a Harlem house.
Then tell them how bad things are down South.

I thought I saw last night
across a ridge,
an ebony bridge that spanned all chasms from
   Harlem to Home.
African!
   Zimbabwe with apartheid still.
   Kenya, prove the Black man's will.
   Biafra, the division is not yet killed.
African!
   Queen's English, manners so defined
   Wardrobe styled and dignified
   Darker skin and no Tarzan smile.
Afro-American!
   Handshake and dashikis too
   James Brown doin' the soul boogaloo
   People starving with nothing to do.
Afro-American!
   Idolizing TV-man
   Capitalism's also-ran
   Colloquialism's cool man.
African! From the continent
Afro-Americans! From the discontent
Brothers! Can we not implement
   a bit of faith?
   a bit of love?
For we are all truly brothers
From the womb of mother same
From the genesis we were one
Let us be one, once again.

ALIEN

Midnight near the border
Tryin' to cross the Rio Grande
Runnin' with coyotes to
Where the streets are paved with gold.

You're diving underwater
When you hear the helicopters
Knowing it's all been less than worthless
(If you meet) the border patrol
Hiding in the shadows
So scared that you want to scream
But you dare not make a sound
If you want to hold on to your dreams.

Hold on! It may not be a lot
Hold on! 'Cause you know it's all you've got
No matter the consequences
Or the fear that grips your senses
You have got to hold on to your dreams.

City of the Angels
With its bright light fascination
Only adds to the confusion
That your mind must now endure.
The 'Gringos' take advantage
When they know that you're illegal
But you avoid La Policia
Like a plague that can't be cured.

Paying the 'mordida'
Lets you know what 'pollos' means

But you dare not file complaints
If you want to hold on to your dreams.

Hold on! It may not be a lot
Hold on! 'Cause you know it's all you've got
No matter the consequences
Or the fear that grips your senses
You have got to hold on to your dreams.

Down at Western Union
Sending cash back to your family
Or drinking down 'cervezas'
Where the lights are very low
Your mind may start to wander
When you think about your village
Or the woman that you love so much
Who's still in Mexico.

At just two bucks an hour
There is little to redeem (this life)
Except that in your mind
You've got to hold on to your dreams

Hold on! It may not be a lot
Hold on! 'Cause you know it's all you've got
No matter the consequences
Or the fear that grips your senses
You have got to hold on to your dreams.

JOHANNESBURG

What's the word?
Tell me brother, have you heard
   from Johannesburg?
What's the word?
Sister/woman have you heard
   from Johannesburg?
   They tell me that our brothers over there
   are defyin' the Man.
We don't know for sure because the news we
   get is unreliable, man.
Well I hate it when the blood starts flowin',
but I'm glad to see resistance growin'.
Somebody tell me what's the word?
Tell me brother, have you heard
   from Johannesburg?
They tell me that our brothers over there
   refuse to work in the mines.
   They may not get the news but they need to know
   we're on their side.
Now sometimes distance brings
   misunderstanding,
but deep in my heart I'm demanding:
Somebody tell me what's the word?
Sister/woman have you heard
   'bout Johannesburg?
I know that their strugglin' over there
ain't gonna free me,
but we all need to be strugglin'
if we're gonna be free.
Don't you wanna be free?

Standing in the ruins of another Black man's life,
Or flying through the valley separating day and
    night.
'I am death,' cried the Vulture. 'For the people
    of the light.'
Charon brought his raft from the sea that sails
    on souls,
And saw the scavenger departing, taking warm
    hearts to the cold.
He knew the ghetto was the haven for the
    meanest creature ever known.
In a wilderness of heartbreak and a desert of
    despair,
Evil's clarion of justice shrieks a cry of naked
    terror.
Taking babies from their mamas and leaving
    grief beyond compare.
So if you see the Vulture coming, flying circles in
    your mind,
Remember there is no escaping for he will
    follow close behind.
Only promise me a battle, battle for your soul
    and mine.

THE REVOLUTION WILL NOT BE TELEVISED

You will not be able to stay home, brother.
You will not be able to plug in, turn on and cop
    out.
You will not be able to lose yourself on scag and
skip out for beer during commercials because
The revolution will not be televised.

The revolution will not be televised.
The revolution will not be brought to you
    by Xerox in four parts without commercial
    interruption.
The revolution will not show you pictures of
    Nixon blowing a bugle and leading a charge by
    John Mitchell, General Abramson and Spiro
    Agnew to eat hog maws confiscated from a
    Harlem sanctuary.
The revolution will not be televised.

The revolution will not be brought to you by
The Schaeffer Award Theatre and will not star
Natalie Wood and Steve McQueen or Bullwinkle
    and Julia?
The revolution will not give your mouth sex
    appeal.
The revolution will not get rid of the nubs.
The revolution will not make you look five
    pounds thinner.
The revolution will not be televised, brother.

There will be no pictures of you and Willie Mae
pushing that shopping cart down the block on
    the dead run

or trying to slide that color tv in a stolen
    ambulance.
NBC will not be able to predict the winner at
    8:32 on reports from twenty-nine districts.
The revolution will not be televised.

There will be no pictures of pigs shooting down
    brothers
on the instant replay.
There will be no pictures of pigs shooting down
    brothers
on the instant replay.
The will be no slow motion or still lifes of Roy
Wilkins strolling through Watts in a red, black
and green liberation jumpsuit that he has been
saving for just the proper occasion.

Green Acres, Beverly Hillbillies and Hooterville
    Junction
will no longer be so damned relevant
and women will not care if Dick finally got down
    with Jane
on *Search for Tomorrow*
because black people will be in the streets
    looking for
A Brighter Day.
The revolution will not be televised.

There will be no highlights on the *Eleven
    O'Clock News*
and no pictures of hairy armed women
    liberationists

and Jackie Onassis blowing her nose.
The theme song will not be written by Jim
    Webb or Francis Scott Key
nor sung by Glen Campbell, Tom Jones, Johnny
    Cash,
Englebert Humperdink or Rare Earth.
The revolution will not be televised.

The revolution will not be right back after a
message about a white tornado, white lightning
    or white people.
You will not have to worry about a dove in your
    bedroom,
the tiger in your tank or the giant in your toilet
    bowl.
The revolution will not go better with Coke.
The revolution will not fight germs that may
    cause bad breath.
The revolution *will* put you in the driver's seat.
The revolution will not be televised
                will not be televised
            not be televised
                be televised
The revolution will be no re-run, brothers.
The revolution will be LIVE.

H₂O GATE (WATERGATE) BLUES – *INTRO*

(as originally recorded on *Winter In America*)

This here, this is gonna be a blues number.
But first I want to do a little bit of background on the blues,
Say what it is:

Like there are six cardinal colors
and colors have always come to signify more
than simply that particular shade
Like 'RED-NECK'
Or 'GOT-THE-BLUES'
That's where you apply colors to something else, you know,
To come up with what it is you're tryin' to say.

There are six cardinal colors –
yellow, red, orange, green, blue and purple.
And there are three thousand shades.
If you take these three thousand shades
and divide them by six,
then you'll come up with five hundred –
meaning there are at least five hundred
shades of the blues.

For example there is the 'I ain't got me no money' blues.
There's the 'I ain't got me no woman' blues.
There's the 'I ain't got me no money and I ain't got me no
    woman blues',
which is the 'double blues'.

And for years it was thought that black people was the only
    ones who could get the blues,

so the blues hadn't come into no international kind of fame.
But lately we had the FRANK RIZZO with the lie detector
    blues;
We had the UNITED STATES GOVERNMENT talking
    about the energy crisis blues;
And we gonna dedicate this next poem here to SPEARHEAD
    X, (Spiro Agnew)
The ex-second-in-command in terms of this country.
And the poem is called H_2O gate blues
And if H_2O is still water and g-a-t-e is still gate
What we gettin' ready to deal on is
The 'Watergate Blues' . . .

H₂O GATE (WATERGATE) BLUES

Click! Whirr . . . Click!
'I'm sorry, the government you have elected is
    inoperative . . .
Click! Inoperative!'
Just how blind will America be?
The world is on the edge of its seat
defeat on the horizon, very surprisin'
that we all could see the plot
and claimed that we could not.
Just how blind, America?
Just how blind, Americans?
Just as Viet Nam exploded in the rice
snap, crackle and pop
could not stop people determined to be free.
The shock of a Viet Nam defeat
sent Republican donkeys scurrying down on
    Wall Street
and when the roll was called it was:
Phillips 66 and Pepsi-Cola plastics,
Boeing Dow and Lockheed –
ask them what we're fighting for
and they never mention the economics of war.
Ecological Warfare! Above all else destroy the
    land!
If we can't break the Asian's will
We'll bomb the dykes and starve the man!

America! The international Jekyll and Hyde,
the land of a thousand disguises
sneaks up but rarely surprises,
plundering the Asian countryside in the name of
    Fu Man Chu.

Just how long, America?
Just how long, Americans?
Who was around where Hale Boggs died?
And what about LBJ's untimely demise?
And whatever happened to J. Edgar Hoover?
The king is proud of Patrick Gray
While America's faith is drowning
   beneath that cesspool – Watergate.

How long will the citizens sit and wait?
It's looking like Europe in '38 and
did they move to stop Hitler before it was too
   late?
How long, America before the consequences of:
allowing the press to be intimidated
keeping the school system segregated
watching the price of everything soar
and hearing complaints 'cause the rich want
   more?
It seems that MacBeth, and not his lady, went
   mad.
We've let him eliminate the whole middle-class.
What really happened to J. Edgar Hoover?
The king is proud of Patrick Gray
while America's faith is drowning
beneath that cesspool – Watergate.

How much more evidence do the citizens need
that the election was rigged with trickery and
   greed?
And, if this is so, and who we got didn't win

let's do the whole Goddam election over again!
The obvious key to the whole charade
would be to run down all the games that they
    played:
Remember Dita Beard and ITT, the slaughter of
    Attica,
the C.I.A. in Chile knowing nothing about
    Allende at this time
in the past. The slaughter in Augusta, G.A.
the nomination of Supreme Court Jesters to
head off the tapes,
William Calley's Executive Interference in the
image of John Wayne,
Kent State, Jackson State, Southern Louisiana,
hundreds of unauthorized bombing raids,
the chaining and gagging of Bobby Seale –
somebody tell these jive Maryland Governors to
    be for real!
We recall all of these events just to prove
that Waterbuggers in the Watergate wasn't no
    news!
And the thing that justifies all our fears
is that all this went down in the last five years.
And what really happened to J. Edgar Hoover?
The king is proud of Patrick Gray
while America's faith is drowning
beneath that cesspool – Watergate.

We leave America to ponder the image of its
    new leadership:
Frank Rizzo, the high school graduate Mayor of
    Philadelphia, whose

ignorance is surpassed only by those who voted
    for him.
Richard Daley, Mayor of Chicago, who took
    over from Al Capone and
continues to implement the same tactics.
Lester Maddawg, George Wallace, Strom
    Thurmond, Ronald Reagan –
an almost endless list that won't be missed
    when at last
America is purged.
And the silent White House with the James
    Brothers once in command.
Sauerkraut Mafia men deserting the sinking
    White House ship and
their mindless, meglomaniac Ahab.
McCord has blown. Mitchell has blown.
No tap on my telephone.
Haldeman, Erlichmann, Mitchell and Dean
It follows a pattern if you dig what I mean.
And what are we left with?
Bumper stickers saying Free the Watergate 500,
spy movies of the same name with a cast of
    thousands,
and that ominous phrase: If Nixon knew, Agnew!
What really happened to J. Edgar Hoover?
The king is proud of Patrick Gray
while America's faith is drowning
beneath that cesspool – Watergate.

WE BEG YOUR PARDON, AMERICA

We beg your pardon, America.
We beg your pardon
because the pardon you gave this time
was not yours to give.
They call it due process and some people are
    overdue.
We beg your pardon, America.
Somebody said 'BrotherMan gon' break a
    window,
gon' steal a hub cap,
gon' smoke a joint and BrotherMan gon' go to
    jail.'
The man who tried to steal America is not in
    jail.
Get caught with a nickel bag, BrotherMan!
Get caught with a nickel bag, SisterLady
on your way to get yo' hair fixed!
You'll do Big Ben and Big Ben is Time.
A man who tried to fix America will not do
    time.
Said they wuz gonna' slap his wrist
and retire him with $850,000.
America was shocked!
America leads the world in shock.
Unfortunately, America doesn't lead the world
in deciphering
the cause of shock.
Eight hundred and fifty thousand dollars they
said and the people protested;
so they said, 'All right, we'll give him $200,000.'
Everybody said, 'Okay, that's better.'

I'd like to retire with $200,000 some day.
San Quentin, not San Clemente!
Go directly to jail, Do not pass Go! Do not
    collect $200,000.
We beg your pardon, America
We beg your pardon
because somehow the pardon did not sit
    correctly,
What were the causes for this pardon?
Well, they had phlebitis.
Rats bite us – no pardon in the ghetto.
They said National Security, but do you feel
secure
with the man who tried to steal America
back on the streets again?
And what were the results of this pardon?
We now have Oatmeal Man.

Anytime you find someone in the middle
Anytime you find someone who is lukewarm
Anytime you find someone
who has been in Congress for twenty-five years
and no one ever heard of him, you've got
    Oatmeal Man.
Oatmeal Man: straddling uncomfortably
yards of barbed wire.
Oatmeal Man: the man who said
you could fit all of his Black friends
in the trunk of his car and still have room
for the Republican elephant.
Oatmeal Man: there was no crime he
    committed.

Oatmeal Man says that, America,
In 1975 your President will
be a 1913 Ford.
Regressive.
Circle up the wagons
to defend
yourself from nuclear attack.
Reminiscent of 1964's Goldwater.
Thank God he didn't win.
But Oatmeal Man didn't win.
I didn't vote for him.
Did you vote for him?

But that's the first result. And the second would
  be:
The dread Rockefeller. Doubtlessly being
  promoted
for the job he did at Attica?
Forty-three dead and millions of Americans
Once again, in shock!
Doubtlessly being promoted for the job he did
  on the streets
of New York City, where the pushers push
  drugs that the
government allows in the country to further
  suppress the masses
who then do time.
They do life or death or life and death
behind bars.
While William Saxbe wanted to dismiss
the Lorton Furlough Program

and Brother Richard X faces 1,365 years
(did he say one thousand three hundred and
    sixty-five years) for participating at Attica.
Rockefeller faces the Vice-Presidency of this
    country
for his participation.
And all is calm and quiet
along the white sands at San Clemente.

We beg your pardon, America.
We beg your pardon, once again
because we found that seven out of every
    ten Black men
are behind bars
(and it seems that seven out of every ten men
    behind bars are Black)
seven out of every ten of these Black men
never went to the 9th grade
and hadn't had a hundred dollars for a month
when they went to jail.
So the poor and the ignorant go to jail
while the rich go to San Clemente.
We beg your pardon, America
because we understand much better than we
    understood before.
But we don't want you to take the pardon back.
We want you to issue some more.
Pardon Brother Frank Willis, the Watergate
    security guard.
He was only doing his job (and now he can't
    find one).

Pardon H. Rap Brown, it was only burglary.
Pardon Robert Vesco, it was only embezzlement.
And pardon us while we get sick.
Because they pardoned William Calley:
twenty-two dead and America in shock.
And as we understand all the better, we beg your
  pardon
as unemployment spirals to seven per cent
(and it seems like seventy per cent in my
  neighborhood)
as we watch cattlemen on tv shoot cows in the
  head
and kick them into graves
while millions are starving in the Sahel?
and Honduras and maybe even next door.
We understand all the more deeply
as Boston becomes Birmingham becomes Little
  Rock becomes Selma, becomes Philadelphia,
    Mississippi
becomes yesterday all over again.
We understand and we beg your pardon.
We beg your pardon, America
because we have an understanding of karma:
what goes around comes around.
We beg your pardon, America
because the pardon you gave this time was not
  yours to give.

THE GHETTO CODE

(DOT-DOT-DIT-DIT-DOT-DOT-DASH)

Communication has always been an important part of our existence. In Africa we were dependent upon the drummer's rhythm to keep us informed and in touch with villages far up the Nile. As captives, in this country, our contact through the drums was destroyed, but not our need to communicate or our need for independent communications.

For the past couple of years, we have seen a totally new Ghetto Code begin to develop. The primary phrase that has caught on from the code has been 'Dot-dot-dit-dit-dot-dot-dash.' It means 'Damned if I know.' Daily there are more and more revelations that make us uncertain of things we thought we were positive about. So: 'Dot-dot-dit-dit-dot-dot-dash.' Damned if I know.

A good example I might give would be Astrology. Lately, more and more people have been re-investigating Astrology – finding out what their signs and their placements are. That was all well and good until folks found out that somebody had been messing with the calendar. They found out that the month in our calendar called July was slipped in to honor Julius Caesar. They found the month called August had been slipped in to honor Augustus Caesar. They found there was a problem with September because it is the Latin word for *seventh*, but it is the *ninth* month in our calendar. And people familiar with the romance languages jumped all over it – octo means eight, but October is the *tenth* month; nove means nine, but November is *eleventh*; and dece means ten, but December is *twelfth*! 'Dot-dot-dit-dit-dot-dot-dash.' Damned if I know.

The problem seems to originate in February. It takes at least thirty days to qualify as a month (the precedent having been established by the other eleven). Yet, February has twenty-eight days three times in a row and if you make the leap year, you get a bonus. 'Dot-dot-dit-dit-dot-dot-dash.' Damned if I know.

There was another problem with the alphabet. Tracing the origins of the symbols, I found that they were called 'Alpha Beta' and contained *all* of these symbols from Alphato Omega – that is from beginning to end. From Alpha – the letter a – the beginning, to Omega – the letter q – the end; but they got nine more letters coming after 'the end.' R-S-T-U-V-W-X-Y-Z. What do I think? 'Dot dot-dit-dit-dot-dot-dash.' Damned if I know!

The letter that has become my favorite is the letter 'c.' It is multipurpose, but it does not receive the proper amount of respect. Highly underrated.

The first letter in Cash.

The first letter in Constitution.

The last letter in musiC.

The first letter in C.I.A.

The C.I.A. and F.B.I., noses pressed against our window panes,

Ears glued to our telephones.

Why won't they leave us alone?

Trying to pick up on . . . the Ghetto Code.

Old fashioned Ghetto codes saw phone
    conversations like this:
'Hey, Bree-is-other me-is-an? You goin' to the
    pe-is-arty to ne-is-ite?'
Oh, yeah! Well, why not bring me a nee-is-ickel
    be-is-ag? You dig?'
I know who ever they was paying at the time to

listen in on my calls had to be scratchin' his head
sayin', 'Dot-dot-dit-dit-dot-dot-dash.' (Damned if
I know!)

But as to the letter 'c.' If it reminds you of cash money, there is a
definite connection. The C.I.A. was responsible for the transfer
of $400,000,000 to one Howard Hughes. This $400,000,000
(give or take a million or two) was to be used for a covert
salvaging mission at sea, to be undertaken by a Hughes seacraft,
the Glo-Mar Challenger. This salvage craft would be used to
recover a Russian submarine that sank in 1968. The reason the
recovery of this submarine was *so* important to our government
was because of the Russian codes on board.

The Russian sub had allegedly broken into three pieces some-
where in the Pacific (which is almost like saying somewhere on
the planet Earth). The Glo-Mar located the sub and proceeded
to salvage it with, we believe, a giant magnet.

The magnet went down and recovered the first third of the
Russian sub, containing some seventy dead Russian sailors. (No
advantage there. Considering the sizeable sum allocated and the
zero rubles put forth by the Kremlin.) The second part of the sub
to be brought to the surface had two Polaris-styled nuclear
warheads on board. (No real advantage there. This country has
already stockpiled sufficient nuclear weapons to have damn
near one bomb for every individual. These recovered Russian
weapons could not have made the $400 million difference.)
Then comes the strange part of the operation. As preparations
were being made to recover the third and final part, the part
with the all-important code books on board, questions began to
bubble to the surface.

'The Russian sub went in 1968, right?'

'We've been trying to find those code books for almost six years now, right?'

'When you lose your code books, don't you change your codes?'

'If they've changed their codes, why did we spend all that money?' 'Dot-dot-dit-dit-dot-dot-dash.' (Damned if I know.)

But perhaps your personal problems do not revolve around cash. Perhaps the 'c' will remind you of Cuba. There was a C.I.A. co-ordinated invasion of Cuba at the Bay of Pigs. The invasion was a total failure, but it did reveal clues that had to do with an assassination attempt on a man whose name starts with 'c' – Castro.

The 'c' might remind you of Chile. Over eight million American dollars were spent there by the C.I.A. to help overthrow and destroy a man named Salvador Allende who just happened to be a 'c' – communist.

The 'c' might remind you of the Canal. The Panama Canal. The covert base established in Panama by the C.I.A. to institute plans for 'c' – Columbia eventually led to the destruction of 'c' – Che Guevara.

The 'c' might remind you of the Congo. The Belgian Congo. Before Zaire was there, there were revolutionary factions brooding in Katanga province. In 1960, there was a statement from a Black leader indicating the possible requeste d'intervention from the Soviet Union shortly before a coup d'etat that left him dead of assassination. His name? Patrice Lumumba.

A string of questions with few answers. Problems with few solutions like: 'Was that Lee Harvey Oswald over there? Or in that corner? Was he 5'8", 165 pounds or 6'2", 205? Was he photographed for his passport in Dallas or was that Moscow?

Arthur Bremmer. Was he from Massachusetts, Michigan or Maryland? Was he captured in the midwest or the Middle East? And if they always have a photo of them before they commit these crimes, why can't they stop them?' 'Dot-dot-dit-dit-dot-dot-dash.' (Damned if I know.)

There seems to have been a stream of too many unanswered questions that always had tracks leading back to the same doorway.

JFK. You believe that?
RFK. You believe that?
MLK. You believe that?
Malcolm X. You believe that?
All some elaborate 'c' – Coincidence?
Or just a little old 'c' – Conspiracy?

There are several questions concerning the letter
'c,' this most important of letters, that most in-
dividuals should be asking themselves:
'The C.I.A. . . . who runs that organization?'
And, 'Who runs this country?'
'Dot-dot-dit-dit-dot-dot-dash.' (Damned if I know!)

Some people think that America invented the blues
and few people doubt that America is the home of the blues.
And the bluesicians have gone all over the world carrying the
blues message and the world has snapped its fingers and
                                                     tapped
its feet right along with the blues folks, but
the blues has always been totally American.
As American as apple pie.
As American as the blues.
As American as apple pie.
The question is why . . .
why should the blues be so at home here?
Well, America provided the atmosphere
America provided the atmosphere for the blues and the blues
                                                  was born.
The blues was born on the American wilderness,
The blues was born on the beaches where the slave ships
                                                  docked,
born on the slave man's auction block
The blues was born and carried on the howling wind.
The blues grew up a slave.
The blues grew up as property.
The blues grew up in Nat Turner visions.
The blues grew up in Harriet Tubman courage.
The blues grew up in small town deprivation.
The blues grew up in the nightmares of the white man.
The blues grew up in the blues singing of Bessie and Billie
                                                and Ma.
The blues grew up in Satchmo's horn, on Duke's piano
in Langston's poetry, on Robeson's baritone.
The point is . . . that the blues is grown.

The blues is grown now – fully grown and you can
    trace
the evolution of the blues on a parallel line
with the evolution of this country.
From Plymouth Rock to acid rock.
From 13 states to Watergate,
The blues is grown, but not the home.
The blues is grown, but the country has not.
The blues remembers everything the country forgot.

It's a Bicentennial year and the blues is
celebrating a birthday, and it's a Bicentennial blues.
America has got the blues and it's a Bicentennial edition.
The blues view may amuse you but make
no mistake – it's a Bicentennial year.
A year of hysterical importance
A year of historical importance:
ripped-off like donated moments from the past.
Two hundred years ago this evening.
Two hundred years ago last evening, and what about now?
The blues is now.
The blues has grown up and the country has not.
The country has been ripped-off!
Ripped-off like the Indians!
Ripped-off like jazz!
Ripped-off like nature!
Ripped-off like Christmas!
Manhandled by media over-kill,
Goosed by aspiring Vice Presidents.
Violated by commercial corporations – A Bicentennial year
The year the symbol transformed into the B-U-Y-centennial.

Buy a car.
Buy a flag.
Buy a map . . . until the public en masse has been
   bludgeoned into
Bicentennial submission
or Bicentennial suspicion.
I fall into the latter category . . .
It's a blues year and America
has got the blues.
It's got the blues because of
partial deification of
partial accomplishments over a
partial period of time.
Half-way justice.
Half-way liberty.
Half-way equality.
It's a half-ass year
and we would be silly in all our knowledge,
in all our self-righteous knowledge
When we sit back and laugh and mock the things
that happen in our lives;
to accept anything less than the truth
about this Bicentennial year.

And the truth relates to two hundred years of
people and ideas getting by!
It got by George Washington!
The ideas of justice, liberty and equality got cold
by George Washington.
Slave owner general!
Ironic that the father of this country

should be a slave owner.
The father of this country a slave owner
having got by him
it made it easy to get by his henchmen,
the creators of this liberty,
who slept in bed with the captains of the slave
    ships,
Fought alongside Black freed men in the Union
    Army,
and left America a legacy of hypocrisy.
It's blues year.
Got by Gerald Ford!

Oatmeal Man.
Has declared himself at odds with people
on welfare . . . people who get food stamps,
day care children, the elderly, the poor, women
    and
people who might vote for Ronald Reagan.
Ronald Reagan — it got by him. Hollyweird!
Acted like an actor
acted like a liberal
acted like General Franco, when he acted like
Governor of California.
Now he acts like somebody might vote for him
    for President.
It got by Jimmy Carter,
'Skippy.'
Got by Jimmy Carter and got by him and his
    friend
the Colonel . . . the creators of southern fried
    triple talk,

A blues trio.
America got the blues.
It got by Henry Kissinger
the international Godfather of peace.
A Piece of Vietnam!
A Piece of Laos!
A Piece of Angola!
A Piece of Cuba!
A blues quartet and America got the blues.
The point is that it may get by you
for another four years
for another eight years . . . you stuck playing
    second fiddle in a blues quartet.
Got the blues looking for the first principle
which was justice.
It's a blues year for justice.
It's a blues year for the San Quentin Six, looking
    for justice.
It's a blues year for Gary Tyler, looking for justice.
It's blues year for Rev. Ben Chavis, looking for
    justice.
It's a blues year for Boston, looking for justice.
It's a blues year for babies on buses,
It's a blues year for mothers and fathers with
babies on buses.
It's a blues year for Boston and it's a blues year
all over this country.
America has got the blues and the blues is
in the street looking for three principles—
justice, liberty, equality.
We would do well to join the blues looking for

justice, liberty, and equality.
The blues is in the street.
America has got the blues but don't let it get by
us.

Hey yeah, we're the same brothers from a long time ago
We was talkin' about television and doin' it on the radio
What we did was to help our generation realize
They got to get out there and get busy
'Coz it wasn't gonna be televised.
We got respect for young rappers and the way they free
                                                    wayin'
But if you goin' to be teaching folks things, be sure you
   know what you sayin'
Older folks in our neighbourhood got plenty of 'know how'
Remember if it wasn't for them
You wouldn't be out there now.
And I ain't coming at you with no disrespect
All I'm sayin' is that you damn well got to be correct.
Because if you goin' to be speaking for a whole generation
Do you know enough to try and handle their education?
Be sure you know the real deal about past situations
And not just repeating what you heard on a local tv station.
Sometimes they tell lies and put 'em in a truthful disguise
But the truth is, that's why we said it wouldn't be *televised*.
They don't know what to say to our young folk
But they know that you do
If they really know the truth,
Why would they tell you?

First sign is peace
Tell all them gun-totin' young brothers
The Man is glad to see us out there killin' one another
We raised too much hell when they were shootin' us down
So they started poisoning our minds and tryin' to jerk us all
                                                    around

102

And then they tell us they've got to come in and control our
                                                    situation
They want half of us on dope, and the other half in
                                                    incarceration.
If the ones they want dead ain't killed by what they instigated
They can put some dope on the brother's body
And claim it was 'drug related'.
Tell 'em 'drug related' means there don't need to be no
                                                    investigation
OK at least that's the way they goin' to play it on the local
                                                    tv station
All you 9 mm brothers,
Give 'em something to think about
Tell 'em you heard, that this is the new word
They got to work that stuff out.
'Coz somehow they feelin' the wrong way with a gun in their
                                                    hands
They feelin' real independent
But they just pullin' contracts for *The Man.*
Live at Five will tell you it's hopeless out there on the avenue
But if they really knew the truth, why would they tell you?
And if they look at you like you're insane
An they start callin' you scarecrow and say you ain't got no
                                                    brain
Or start tellin' folks that you suddenly gone lame
Or that white folks have finally co-opted your game
Or worse yet, implying that you don't really know
That's the same thing they said about us a long time ago.

Young rappers, one more suggestion before I get out of your
                                                    way

103

But I appreciate the respect you give me and what you got to
say.
I'm sayin' protect your community and spread that respect
around
Tell brothers and sisters they got to calm that bullshit down
Coz we terrorizing our old folks and we bought fear into our
homes
And they ain't got to hang out with the senior citizens
Just tell 'em damn it, leave the old folks alone.
And we know who's ripping off the neighborhood
Tell 'em, that bullshit has got to stop
Tell 'em, you sorry they can't handle it out there
But they got to take the crime off the block.
And if they look at you like they think you're insane
Or start calling you scarecrow thinkin' you ain't got no brain
Or start telling folks that you suddenly gone lame
Or that white folks have suddenly co-opted your game
Or worse yet saying that you really don't know
That's the same thing they said about me a long time ago.
And if they tell folks that you finally lost your nerve
That's the same thing they said about us
When we said 'Johannesburg'.
But I think you young folks need to know things don't go
both ways
You can't talk respect on every other song or just every other
day.
What I'm speaking on now is the raps about the womenfolks
On one song she your African queen, and on the next one
she's a joke.
And you ain't said no words that I haven't heard
But that ain't no compliment

It only insults eight people out of ten and questions your
                                        intelligence
Four letter words or four syllable words won't make you a
                                                poet
It will only magnify how shallow you are and let everybody
                                        know it.
If they look at you like they think you're insane
Or they call you scarecrow thinkin' you ain't got no brain
Or start tellin' folks that you suddenly gone lame
Or that the white folks have finally co-opted your game
Or you really don't know
They said that about me a long time ago.
If they finally start to tell people that you lost your nerve
Thats what they said about Johannesburg.
You *ain't* insane
You *have* got a brain
You *haven't* gone lame
You *have* got your game
Remember, keep the nerve
We're talkin' 'bout peace.

SPEED KILLS

Speed on by. Don't seem to have the time.
What about this life, what about this life
Can I call mine?
Issues in the paper, but somehow I'm not concerned.
Seems I've been this way before, but I never learn.
Children slowly turn.

Time sped gone. We didn't see it go.
Now what do we have, now what do we have
That we can show?
Friends you swore you'd never lose melted from your style
Down the tunnels of your youth and now you never smile.
Children learn to smile.

I have believed in my convictions
and been convicted for my beliefs.
I have been conned by the Constitution
and harassed by the police.
I have been billed for the Bill of Rights
as though I'd done something wrong.
I have become a special amendment
for what included me all along.
Like: 'All men are created equal.'
(No amendment needed there)
I've contributed in every field including cotton
from Sunset Strip to Washington Square.
Back during the non-violent era
I was the only non-violent one.
Come to think of it there was no non-violence
'cause too many rednecks had guns.
There seems to have been this pattern
that took a long time to pick up on.
But all black leaders who dared stand up
wuz in jail, in the courtroom or gone.
Picked up indiscriminately
by the shocktroops of discrimination
to end up in jails or tied up in trials
while dirty tricks soured the nation.
I've been hoodwinked by professional hoods,
My ego had happened to me.
'Just keep things cool!' they kept repeating.
'And keep the people out of the streets.
We'll settle all this at the conference table.
You leave everything to me.'
Which brings me back to my convictions

and being convicted for my beliefs
'cause I believe these smiles
in three piece suits
with gracious, liberal demeanor
took our movement off the streets
and took us to the cleaners.
In other words, we let up the pressure
and that was all part of their plan
and every day we allow to slip through our fingers
is playing right into their hands.

Tuskeegee #626
Somebody done got slick
When deadly germs are taking turns
Seeing what makes us tick

Tuskeegee #626
Scientists getting their kicks
When deadly disease can do what it please
Results ain't hard to predict

Tuskeegee #626
Pushed aside mighty quick
When brothers, you dig
Are guinea pigs
For vicious experiments.

The King is alive and twenty millions strong
And long before he ever ascended to the throne
He was made fun of, a source of great humor
His domination over neighborhoods was nothing but a rumor
Back when the King's name was so rarely spoke
And the ten million disciples mentioned by some folks
Was called exaggerated and treated like a joke
They didn't understand that the monster had woke
But the King could instantly demonstrate
That he wasn't no laughing matter
Blow folks away so quickly it would demonstrate
Nobody and nothing does it better
Now we're talking about total finesse
That's when you know you're dealing with the best
There ain't even been one whisper of force
Over the entire kingdom of Henry IV

The awful thing about it is there ain't nothing you can do
Guard all your doors and windows and the King can still
                rob you
Oh, No! ain't talking about the '60s, not that f'n far back
In the '80s with folks falling into and between the cracks
And talking about being right in the center of the news
But the King don't never give no interviews
And the reporters was lined up. The King was raising hell
              around here
And then information just dried up and the king seemed to
              disappear
Gone so quickly you might have just an impression
Moved along so slickly it was like an amnesia expression
Am I certain of my facts now of course.
I know almost all there is to know about King Henry IV

What it left on the ghetto streets was an incorrect
                                        understanding
About the ways he caught on and how rapidly he was
                                        expanding
The reason I felt black kids was headed for a fall
Was the day I read this poem painted in a bathroom stall:
Fuck a man in the butt and you could get it for sure
Pass a dope needle around and there wasn't no cure
The kids believed if you wasn't gay and didn't shoot dope
You was home free, take the day off and float
But what would always make the King seem so tough
Is that he could get in and then take five years to show back up
And you can go scream at them until you get hoarse
But they don't understand and about King Henry IV

[There was only Public Enemy with really decent shit to say
And maybe Run DMC had it with 'Walk This Way'
15 years ago? Hell it wasn't even ten
Which only goes to show how fast the King is moving in]

He was no more than a whisper at gay after-hours spots
If there are no bloodless revolutions why hadn't he fired a
    shot?
Sunday mornings from the pulpit he was blamed on
    promiscuity
More confusing newspaper bullshit only furthered the
    ambiguity
Preacher's became obsessed and called him a message from
    above
The creature's game progressed since nobody knew who the
    fuck he was

111

Completely taking over areas that had never seen royalty
But soon millions on five continents could all pledge their
  loyalty
The invisible monarch was steady doing his thing
He never heard folks once saying 'Hail to the King!'
But he's got powers you can't help but endorse
And the Africans call him King Henry IV

A POEM FOR JOSE CAMPOS TORRES

I had said I wasn't gonna' write no more poems
   like this.
I had confessed to myself all along, tracer of
   life/poetry trends,
that awareness/consciousness poems that screamed
   of pain
and the origins of pain and death had blanketed
   my tablets and therefore
my friends/brothers/sisters/outlaws/in-laws
and besides, they already knew.
But brother Torres,
common, ancient bloodline brother Torres,
is dead.
I had said I wasn't gonna write no more poems
   like this.
I had said I wasn't gonna write no more words
   down
about people kickin' us when we're down
about racist dogs that attack us and
drive us down, drag us down and beat us down.
But the dogs are in the street!
The dogs are alive and the terror in our hearts
   has scarcely diminished.
It has scarcely brought us the comfort we
   suspected:
the recognition of our terror,
and the screaming release of that recognition
has not removed the certainty of that knowledge.
How could it?
The dogs, rabid, foaming with the energy of their
   brutish ignorance,

stride the city streets like robot gunslingers, and
    spread death
as night lamps flash crude reflections from gun
    butts and police shields.

I had said I wasn't gonna' write no more poems
    like this.
But the battlefield has oozed away from the
    stilted debates of
semantics, beyond the questionable flexibility of
    primal screaming.
The reality of our city/jungle streets and their
    gestapos has
become an attack on home/life/family/
    philosophy/total.
It is beyond a question of the advantages of
    didactic niggerisms.
The MOTHERFUCKIN' DOGS are in the street!
In Houston maybe someone said Mexicans were
the new niggers.
In L.A. maybe someone decided Chicanos were
    the new niggers.
In Frisco maybe someone said Asians were the
    new niggers.
Maybe in Philadelphia and North Carolina they
    decided they
didn't need no new niggers.

I had said I wasn't gonna' write no more poems like this.
But the dogs are in the street.
It's a turn around world where things all too
    quickly turn around.

114

It was turned around so that right looked wrong.
It was turned around so that up looked down.
It was turned around so that those who marched
   in the streets
with Bibles and signs of peace became enemies
   of the state
and risks to National Security;
So that those who questioned the operations of
   those in authority
on the principles of justice, liberty, and equality
   became the vanguard of a communist attack.
It became so you couldn't call a spade a
   motherfuckin' spade.
Brother Torres is dead.
The Wilmington Ten are still incarcerated.
Ed Davis, Ronald Reagan and James Hunt and
   Frank Rizzo are still alive.
And the dogs are in the MOTHERFUCKIN' street.
I had said I wasn't gonna' write no more poems
   like this.
I made a mistake.

DON'T GIVE UP (THE SPIRITS)

I never thought of myself as a complex man
Or as someone who was really that hard to understand
Though it would hardly take a genius to realize
I've always been a lot too arrogant and a little too f'n wise
A combination that made a lotta folks duty bound
To do whatever they could to try and bring me down
To head off some of the things I might say
To see if they couldn't take some of my stride away
To bring me disappointment and teach me to fear it
Obviously these are folks who don't have the spirits:

Don't give up. It's time to stop your falling.
You've been down long enough. Can't you hear the spirits
    calling?
It's the spirits can't you hear it calling your name?

There are people whose lives are so far off the track
That what they like best is stabbing brothers in the back
And I was obviously too blind and probably too weak
To see who was responsible for my losing streak
But the best way to explain it is to say simply because
I was looking around outside and truth is that I was the one
So I got locked into all the analysis
And found myself blocked into a kind of paralysis
And something was calling and I almost didn't hear it
But I've spent a lotta time being blessed by the spirits:

Don't give up. It's time to stop your falling.
You've been down long enough. Can't you hear the spirits
    calling?
It's the spirits can't you hear it calling your name?

116

It don't matter whether it was a child or an adult
There was absolutely no one I couldn't insult.
So that I could isolate myself somewhere off to the side
And continue to juggle all the possible 'whys'
The warmth I once could generate so well
Had turned into a frozen hell.
And all of the discouraging injustices I felt
Pinned me inside a drug-infested cell
Where those who told didn't know and those that knew
    didn't tell
And I could continue to feel sorry for myself:

Don't give up. It's time to stop your falling.
You've been down long enough. Can't you hear the spirits
    calling?

Ain't no way overnight to turn your life around.
And this ain't the conversation of someone who never falls
    back down
But no matter how long you've been on trial
With the days of self denial
And no matter how many times you tried to make it
And found out that right then you just couldn't take it
If you're looking for a loser who found strength and success
Remember the spirit of brother Malcolm X
And know that you can leave all of your mistakes behind
The day you really make up your mind:

Don't give up. It's time to stop your falling.
You've been down long enough. Listen to the spirits calling!

PUBLICATIONS

1 *The Vulture* (novel), 1970, World Publishing; 1996, Payback Press
2 *Small Talk at 125th & Lenox* (poetry), 1970, World Publishing
3 *The Nigger Factory*, (novel), 1972 The Dial Press; 1996, Payback Press
4 *The Mind of Gil Scott-Heron* (poetry booklet/LP), 1979, Arista
5 *So Far, So Good* (poetry), 1990, Third World Press
6 *Now and Then* (poetry) 2000, Payback Press/Brouhaha Books

RECORDINGS

1 *Small Talk at 125th & Lenox*, 1970, Flying Dutchman Records
2 *Pieces of a Man*, 1971, Flying Dutchman
3 *Free Will*, 1972, Flying Dutchman
4 *Winter In America*, 1974, Strata-East
5 *The Revolution Will Not Be Televised* (compilation), 1974, Flying Dutchman
6 *First Minute of a New Day*, 1975, Arista
7 *From South Africa to South Carolina*, 1975, Arista
8 *It's Your World*, 1976, Live Double LP set, Arista
9 *Bridges*, 1977, Arista
10 *Secrets*, 1978, Arista
11 *The Mind of Gil Scott-Heron*, 1979, Arista
12 *1980*, 1980, Arista
13 *Real Eyes*, 1980, Arista
14 *Reflections*, 1981, Arista
15 *Moving Target*, 1982, Arista
16 *The Best of Gil Scott-Heron*, 1984, Arista
17 *Space Shuttle*, 1989, Castle Communication
18 *Tales of the Amnesia Express* [Live], 1990, Castle Communication
19 *Glory* [compilation], 1992, Arista-Ariola
20 *Spirits*, 1994, TVT Records

The Vulture & The Nigger Factory
Gil Scott-Heron

Gil Scott-Heron's highly successful two novels are now collected together for the first time.

A hip and fast moving thriller, *The Vulture* relates the strange story of John Lee's murder – telling it in the words of four men who knew him when he was just another kid, working after school, hanging out, and waiting for something to happen. Just who did kill John Lee, and why?

The Nigger Factory is a scornful statement on the way which human beings are conditioned to think. On the campus of Sutton University, Virginia, the students are trying to carry forth the message of reconstruction to a university resistant to change. The failure of Sutton to embrace the changing attitudes of the Sixties has necessiated extreme reaction, and the revolution is nigh . . .

'They are impressive and ambitious works that vigorously mix street savvy and intellectual flair. They retain a freshness and energy that has dated them little.'   *GQ*

'With the pace of cleanly constructed thrillers they wield the force of a highly focused political consciousness.'   *The Herald*

'There's plenty of tension and sex, but also a whole heap of politics. These are ace period pieces.'   *Select*

'They're prodigious works, displaying the ability with words that his subsequent recorded works show so clearly.'   *Wire*

The Vulture & The Nigger Factory
ISBN 0 86241 901 8
£7.99 pbk

Buy online at www.canongate.net for a 20% discount.

Payback Poetry

Rebel Without Applause – Lemn Sissay
The long-awaited reprint of Lemn Sissay's debut collection.
'Fierce, funny, serious, satirical, streetwise and tender.'
The Big Issue
ISBN 1 8419 6 001 7
£7.99 pbk

Morning Breaks in the Elevator – Lemn Sissay
This is a twist of Lemn. His first solo collection in eight years.
'Easily the best, most comprehensive collection of poetry about
modern Britain I have read for a long time.'
Straight No Chaser
ISBN 0 86241 838 9
£7.99 pbk

The Fire People – Edited by Lemn Sissay
A coming together of the finest contemporary Black British poets,
including Tricky, Jackie Kay and Linton Kwesi Johnson.
'The collection forms a milestone of great significance.'
The Times
ISBN 0 86241 739 2

Transformatrix – Patience Agbabi
Inspired by '90s poetry, '80s rap and '70s disco, *Transformatrix* is
an exploration of women, travel and the realties of modern Britain.
'Rising Star . . . Patience Agbabi.'
The Observer
ISBN 0 86241 941 7
£7.99 pbk

Buy online at www.canongate.net for a 20% discount.

,